GUSTAVE
CAILLEBOTTE

Bonfini

GUSTAVE
CAILLEBOTTE

ERIC DARRAGON

Translation from the French:
Marie-Hélène Agüeros

Color separation:
Fotolito Interscan, Milan

Printed in Italy - Poligrafiche Bolis S.P.A., Bergamo
© 1994 - Bonfini Press Establishment, Vaduz, Liechtenstein
ISBN: 0-568-00244-X

Table of contents

Pink Azalea
in a Clay Pot, n.d.
Oil on canvas
16⅛" × 10⅝" (41 × 27 cm)
Private collection
Photo Galerie Brame et
Lorenceau, Paris

Chapter one

The two faces of a firm belief

In his authoritative book on Claude Monet, the critic and art historian Gustave Geffroy gave a lively account of the personality of the painter Gustave Caillebotte, whose work is now held in high esteem after a long period of relative lack of interest. His realism calls for further reflection and the part he played in it seems crucial to the history of Impressionism. Caillebotte's contribution as an artist as well as a collector and patron covered a span of only a few years, but without it Impressionism would have been deprived of one of its fundamental components. He was at the center of a group, putting forward a number of strongly original ideas at a significant time. Although Caillebotte was a decisive actor in the history of art and he painted pictures which are remembered as archetypal images of modern times, he remained little known or even unknown. Before we analyze his artistic achievement, which was underestimated in the very name of the realism he helped to define, we should follow Gustave Geffroy in an attempt to capture the personality of a painter who found his freedom in discussions with his artist friends. Caillebotte put his firm beliefs and keen mind into these talks. The scene recalls his late years and the celebrated monthly dinners held at the Café Riche between 1890 and 1894, which brought together Claude Monet, Camille Pissarro, Auguste Renoir, Alfred Sisley, the collector Georges de Bellio, the art critics Théodore Duret and Octave Mirbeau, and occasionally the poet Stéphane Mallarmé. The conversation between these men, most of whom had already produced a number of works, resembled a contest in words in which they all regained "the lively spirits of students on the loose".

Some of them had a long experience of this sort of coffee-house discussion. It is important to note that Caillebotte was one of the butts of Renoir's wit in these discussions. Auguste Renoir was an artist by definition, in all his being, his paradoxes and sudden outbursts. Caillebotte was of a more stable nature, with a more rational mind, and he received the full blow of Renoir's spirited wit. He felt a special affection for Renoir, whom he helped financially and whose works he collected.[1] In the end, Caillebotte would get angry: "The tone of the argument would occasionally rise, especially between Renoir and Caillebotte. The former — excitable and sarcastic, with a mocking voice and a sort of mephistophelian mind which imparted an expression of irony and a strange laughter to a face already tormented by illness — took great pleasure in exciting the latter — sanguine and irritable, whose face turned from red to purple and even black when his opinions were contradicted by Renoir's witty remarks. He then showed a passion which could lead to anger, but which nonetheless remained harmless.[2]

These sessions must have entertained everybody since we are told that the painter of *The Ball at the Moulin de la Galette* prepared for each evening's discussion by consulting an encyclopedia beforehand: "The debate covered opinions on art and painting, but also on all matters of literature, politics, and philosophy. Caillebotte, who read a wide range of books, journals and newspapers, put all his good faith in the debate. Renoir kept abreast of everything by buying an encyclopedia in which he found arguments to 'best Caillebotte'." Thus Caillebotte, who died young at the age of forty-five, was described as an honest man with a broad and clear mind, who could be teased, shocked, aroused, and contradicted in his opinions of people and things.

Renoir claimed that he did not know one day what he would do the next. Caillebotte wrote a will in 1876, at the age of twenty-eight, and until his death he stood by a firm decision which was bound to have long-term consequences. Had it not been for his beliefs and the reasonable faith he put in the society of his time, Caillebotte would not have had the necessary energy to paint his pictures. His works remained tied to certain ideas about life and creativity. They seem to be supported by a general philosophy and personal ethics. A letter to Monet dated July 18, 1884 — at a time when Caillebotte was becoming less productive — provides a revealing insight. While he was staying at Trouville, Caillebotte read the letters of Gustave Flaubert, a writer whom the realist painters particularly admired. But these letters reflect an obsession with universal stupidity and, reading them, he felt deeply hurt and dispirited: "This is totally discouraging.' — It killed me to read them."[3] He claimed to be crushed by the void which Flaubert

1. When he died, Caillebotte had eight paintings by Renoir in his collection: *The Reader* (1874), *A Ball at the Moulin de la Galette* (1876), *The Swing* (1876), *Banks of the Seine at Champrosay* (1876), *Woman in the Sun* (1876), *Place Saint-Georges* (ca 1878), *The Railway Bridge at Chatou* (1881), and *Sunset at Montmartre*.

2. Gustave Geffroy, *Claude Monet, sa vie, son temps, son œuvre*. Paris: Crès, 1922, vol. II, pp. 1-2.

3. *Ibid.*, pp. 37-38.

observed everywhere. As if to find an antidote, he called to mind the example of Eugène Delacroix, who, while he also suffered from the stupidity of his contemporaries, excluded it from his work: "As an artist, he is above this, he is Olympian." The remark helps one to understand the anger provoked by Renoir's devilish arguments. Caillebotte respected certain values, which he perceived in such painters as Jean-François Millet: to maintain the level of art, not to lose one's way and be taken unaware by conflicts and polemics, to keep firmly to the essential. According to him, however, "Degas

Garden at Trouville
1880-1882
Oil on canvas
10¾" × 14" (27.5 × 35.5 cm)
Private collection

is not Olympian, and this is a terrible shortcoming." He bared his mind to Monet, at the risk of seeming a bore, because he was pleading for a cause. He was trying to encourage an easily dispirited friend. Implicitly, he was calling on the role Monet had played in the Impressionist exhibitions. He wanted to keep on believing although he knew it was not possible any more. The *Self-Portrait* painted in 1892, two years before he died, shows a man of earnest and almost bitter dignity (see page 10). The time for great statements had passed. Caillebotte observed himself with clear-minded stoicism. He was obviously worn out by a sort of nervous strain. His energy had dried up and he wore the painful mask of experience. The artist used his favorite color scheme in a classical frame, but this classical frame was still in defiance of academic rules. There is a protest and an independence in this picture, whose intensity recalls unexpectedly the violence of Paul Cézanne.

Self-Portrait, 1892
Oil on canvas
15¾" × 12⅝" (40 × 32 cm)
Musée d'Orsay, Paris
Photo Réunion des
Musées nationaux, Paris

There is also another Caillebotte, one in photographs where his lively eyes, his resolute posture and youthful energy are both attractive and inviting. He also painted himself facing the viewer, in full light, smiling: a short moment taken from his studies after nature, which reveals the intellectual, ethical and social structure that was Caillebotte's strength and torment. He was very clear-minded as he entered the world of art — of great art — and he could rely only on his intelligence.

Self-Portrait
With Summer Hat
Before 1879
Oil on canvas
17 ¼" × 13" (44 × 33 cm)
Private collection
Photo Galerie Brame et
Lorenceau, Paris

4. Ca 1879-1880, private
collection, Paris.

Self-Portrait at the Easel,[4] with the motif of Renoir's *Moulin de la Galette* reversed because it is reflected in the mirror before which the artist was standing, brings us directly into the realistic dimension where Caillebotte could give the full measure of his courageous originality: an optical reality synonymous with discovery.

Let us follow Monet and Geffroy along the pilgrimage they made together to the house at Petit-Gennevilliers, where Caillebotte settled in 1887. They may have wanted to fulfill the wishes of a man who had said a little earlier: "You will see my garden in the spring." The visitors saw the house again, its cheerfulness "between the fields and the Seine", and the garden "which kept the appointment punctually." Monet had come to see the garden that was Caillebotte's passion. Like Mirbeau, Caillebotte had a gift for growing flowers; gardening had been a pleasure, an art of life, a path to wisdom. It also helps one to understand his art.

Dahlias, the Garden at Petit-Gennevilliers brings to mind a world in which the significance of the flowers dominates the vista on the greenhouse and the house itself.[5] The dog and the female figure give no access to an elusive intimacy. Monet and Geffroy noted that Caillebotte had marked his presence in a world of order and light which was his. When he died, there disappeared with him an aspect of Impressionism, to which he had given everything. This feeling of accomplishment may create some melancholy and mystery but it also imparts a particular intensity to the appreciation of Caillebotte's role in a history which continued without him. He was reduced to that which he was. Geffroy would note his place as a "pictorial chronicler of modern life", mentioning his series of views of Parisian streets as "the beginning of something which could be pursued". He saluted the incomparable companion and earnest collector.

Today, the *Floor-Scrapers* of 1875 (see pages 30-31) contribute to a better understanding of the fate of the *Stone Breakers* by Gustave Courbet[6] and the *Gleaners* by Millet.[7] In 1877, *Paris Street, Rainy Day* (see pages 60-61) foretold the story of *A Sunday Afternoon on the Island of Grande Jatte* by Georges Seurat.[8] In 1876, *Young Man at the Window* (see page 37) told a story made possible by Manet's *Balcony*.[9] Caillebotte's fate was marked by evidence of fact and logical necessity. This in itself may be a matter to explore. Let us examine the reality in Caillebotte's paintings as it was cropped to an exact representation of the present and is thus viewed by art historians.

5. 1893, private collection, California.

6. Salon of 1850-1851. Formerly at the Museum of Dresden, the painting was destroyed.

7. Salon of 1857, Musée d'Orsay, Paris.

8. 1884-1886, The Art Institute of Chicago. Collection Helen Birch Bartlett.

9. 1868-1869, Musée d'Orsay, Paris.

Dahlias. The House at Petit-Gennevilliers, 1893
Oil on canvas
45¾" × 35½"
(116 × 90 cm)
Private collection

Study for Portrait of
Paul Hugot, ca 1878
Pencil
18¼" × 11⅞" (46 × 30 cm)
Private collection
Photo Galerie Brame et
Lorenceau, Paris

Chapter two

Becoming an Impressionist: the exhibition of 1876

Chronology is important here because Gustave Caillebotte was born in 1848 and belonged to a different generation from that of Degas, Manet, and Pissarro.   Monet was eight years his senior and Renoir seven.   In the group he was to join, he was — like Giuseppe De Nittis, born in 1846, Jean Béraud, born in 1849, Henri Gervex, born in 1852 — a young artist following the example of those who had lived through the decisive years of the Realist movement.   He died at the age of forty-five but, in his relatively short life, he produced major works during a span of a few years and he did not leave the feeling of an effort brutally interrupted.   His story could not be compared to that of Frédéric Bazille or Seurat.   Caillebotte fulfilled his life and this impression is based on a whole body of work marked by consistent originality.   He made history and his determination must be recognized within a certain framework.   One may wonder whether he needed this collective framework and felt at a loss when the ties of Impressionism began to unravel.   Caillebotte never spoke his mind clearly on this matter but his work provides the answer.   The fire died down, after it had shone with great brilliance.

It is appropriate to insist on Caillebotte's social background, his education and his circle because they provided so much of his inspiration.   Although he was exceptional in being wealthy, he shared with many of his future artist friends firm roots in a bourgeois world.   This was a world which made it both possible and necessary for them to be independent.

The Yerres Valley, 1877
Pastel, 22½" × 27⅝"
(57.2 × 70.2 cm)
Private collection

His father, Martial Caillebotte, had been widowed twice and he was forty-nine years old when Gustave was born.   His mother, Céleste Daufresne, was the daughter of a lawyer from Lisieux.   His brother René was born in 1850, followed by Martial in 1853.   Both brothers were to hold a significant place in the artists work.   The family's wealth came from a successful business supplying cloth and blankets to the French army.   The family store, " Le Lit militaire ", was at 160 Rue du Faubourg Saint-Denis, in an older part of Paris; in 1850, it moved to No. 152 in the same street, where the family settled in a large one-family house with a garden.   Caillebotte's father was subsequently awarded the Legion of Honor and he continued on his social ascent as he served as a judge on the Commercial Court of the Seine.   In 1860 he purchased a beautiful country house at Yerres, in the Seine-et-Oise district, close to Paris and in a particularly pleasant area.   In 1868, he left the Rue du Faubourg Saint-Denis and moved to a town house in a newly built residential section of the city, at 77 Rue de Miromesnil, near the Boulevard Malesherbes, on the corner of the Rue de Lisbonne in the eighth *arrondissement*.   This was the Quartier de l'Europe, so called because many of the streets bear the names of European capitals, where the artist was to find most of the themes for his paintings.

Caillebotte had an excellent education in the liberal arts at the Lycée Louis-le-Grand and he received his bachelor's degree in law in April 1869.   After a brief period of military service in 1869, his family purchased a replacement to serve for him from June 1869 to June 1870, while he continued his studies.   He received his law degree on July 23, 1870, at the age of twenty-two.   Shortly thereafter he was called up for active duty for nine months in the Garde mobile of the Seine district.   Napoleon II had declared war against Prussia and Caillebotte experienced the grief of war and the insurgency and bloody defeat of the Paris Commune.   After the war, he decided against a career in law and enrolled in the studio of the painter Léon Bonnat.   He prepared for the entrance examination to the École des Beaux-Arts and was admitted in March 1873.   He had shown a predilection for drawing at an early age and it can be reasonably assumed that he had already had some practice when he decided to pursue a career in painting.

Caillebotte had made a judicious choice in studying under Bonnat: Léon Bonnat was able to give him a solid technical training enriched by his vast culture, acquired in Italy in particular, where he was a friend of Pierre Delaunay, Jean-Jacques Henner, and Edgar Degas.   Around 1862-1863, Degas had painted a portrait of Bonnat and one of his notebooks of 1871 bears the mention of Caillebotte's name. Bonnat was about to become famous for his portraits of celebrities; he did not share the spirit of exclusion displayed by his associates on the jury for the Salon. His realism showing the influence of Spanish painters and a reverent admiration for Dominique Ingres could be a source of fruitful reflection for Caillebotte. Bonnat's culture and good taste must have appealed to the young and distinguished Caillebotte, but the latter had already decided not to follow his master's inspiration. Few early studies are still extant. Some copies in oils after plaster models show a careful rendering of shapes under a glaring light.

His trip to Italy, probably in 1872, was the mark of a thorough training, but other evidence of this, such as copies of old masters, notebooks of drawings and nude studies, is lacking. The painting called *A Road Near Naples*[10] is intriguing, as it seems the work of an already confirmed realist painter; its theme recalls the inspiration of the Italian painter De Nittis, who was a friend of Degas and Manet and exhibited *The Road in Apulia Near Brindisi* at the Salon of 1872. Caillebotte's painting raises a curious problem of interpretation; it shows an artist with a hat, at work behind the frame of his picture, his back turned toward the landscape of the Vesuvius. Whether this scene was staged or really observed, it was an original composition with a characteristic tonal effect. Here, Caillebotte's Italy appears as a touristic setting only and the painter was more interested in exploring an optical relationship with the depiction as such.

The pastel drawing dated 1873, *Reclining Nude*, is interesting for its masterly technique, the subtle virtuosity in the flesh tones and the texture of different fabrics, and — most of all — a composition combining the realism in the woman's posture with an underlying classicism. The nude never became a significant theme in Caillebotte's work, but this drawing stands half-way between Bazille and Degas.

Interior of a Studio with Stove, dated around 1872-1874, is a good example of the beginnings of an artist who had assimilated brilliantly the tradition of romantic realism (see page 20-21). Aside from the reference to the spirit of the years 1850-1860, this interior puts together a few revealing objects: The small copy in plaster of Jean-Antoine Houdon's anatomical model is given pride of place; this proof of seriousness comes to terms with an interest in things Japanese, expressed here by an earthenware bowl, a lantern, and several prints. The framed painting seems a solid study of an exotic figure and forms a

10. 1872, private collection, Paris.

deliberate contrast with two rectangular slanting panels in a Japanese style. The studio presents a body of information expressing a feeling of firm belief. The canvas leaning face to the wall bears the artist's initials on the back. The message conveyed was that Caillebotte could not be distracted from his fixed goal by anything but art and study.

A few observations regarding Caillebotte's approach and personality are necessary before it is possible to examine the manner in which he came to the eyes of the public and the critics in 1876, and from this date until 1882 on the occasion of the

Reclining Nude, 1873
Pastel
34 ¼" × 44 ½" (87 × 113 cm)
Iris and B. Gerald Cantor
Collection

Interior of a Studio
With Stove, ca 1872-1874
Oil on canvas
31⅞" × 25⅝" (81 × 65 cm)
Private collection
Photo Galerie Brame et
Lorenceau, Paris

Impressionist exhibitions. Impressionism — both the word and the fact — already existed during the years when Caillebotte was preparing for his life as a painter. He was to take part in a historical development which had started without him in April 1874 — when he was twenty-six years old — but, most of all, had

Study for
The Floor-Scrapers, ca 1875
Pencil
18⅞" × 12¼" (48 × 31 cm)
Private collection
Photo Galerie Brame et
Lorenceau, Paris

existed before this landmark exhibition through works, discussions, and writings throughout the 1860s. It should also be noted that from 1872 on, the official Salon was more than ever the road any young artist seeking recognition needed to take. Philippe de Chennevières, who was appointed director of the Beaux-Arts in 1873, attempted reforms which raised some hopes but remained inconclusive. The views of the jury reflected the values of order characteristic of the political spirit of the period. While Caillebotte's personal wealth made it economically less pressing, it was natural that the student of Léon Bonnat should send his work to the jury and try to be accepted at the Salon. Bonnat held a most important official position. In 1865 he had painted *Saint Vincent-de-Paul Switching Places With a Convict* in the Church Saint-Nicolas-des-Champs in Paris; he was a member of the jury in 1872 and 1873, and he chaired the jury in 1874, when he exhibited his *Christ* commissioned for the Court House in Paris; he showed the *Portrait of Madame Pasca* at the Salon of 1875, he was to show his renowned *Portrait of Adolphe Thiers* in 1877, and he was on the jury of 1876. The time was near when he would commission Pierre Puvis de Chavannes for the decoration of his town house in the Rue Bassano. He was a friend of Degas and an important collector, whose paintings and drawings — Rembrandt, Rubens, Boticelli, Ingres, Leonardo da Vinci — are now at the museum bearing his name in the city of Bayonne, in the south west of France. While Caillebotte differed markedly from his master, if only on a social level — Bonnat was climbing the social ladder and amassing his fortune — he found an example in the moral personality of Bonnat.

The *Floor-Scrapers* were probably submitted to the jury of the Salon in 1875 and they were rejected. This was the Salon where Manet's *Argenteuil*[11] prompted a violent reaction, and where the works of Béraud were shown, as well as those of De Nittis, Antoine Guillemet, Henri Fantin-Latour, Marcellin Desboutin, Alphonse Legros, Eugène Boudin, and Corot, who had died recently. It is interesting to examine the *Floor-Scrapers* in this light. It has been noted that the signature and the date were painted very large but, more importantly, that it illustrates the theme of the nude, more precisely nude torsos in an interior scene whose harmony was made of light and sparseness. This rejection must have offended Caillebotte in his beliefs and strengthened his already existing faith in an independent realism. He joined the other "intransigents" and, having learned his lesson, he never submitted another work to the jury. The question remains whether his picture benefited from Bonnat's experienced advice and approval. It may have, as it possesses technical qualities showing an energy and seriousness which would be recognized and encouraged in a beginner. In spite of all the interesting formal characteristics of this painting and the others he showed in 1876, he did not establish that he belonged entirely to a school of

11. 1874, Musée des Beaux-Arts, Tournai, Belgium.

painting after nature, with bright colors and divided brushstrokes. The experience may have been short but it could be said that Caillebotte's early efforts reflected a sincere desire to be part of the Salon and that his failure to do so opened the way to his further artistic development.

This first major work impresses the viewer with the fact also that from the very beginning Caillebotte displayed the qualities which were very much his own. He did so with great directness, without trying to prove that he was someone's student or the heir to a tradition. Not only was his originality significant by itself but it revealed also the absence of any eclecticism, any assimilation of knowledge based on the use of models or references. An excerpt from Delacroix's "Diary" — then unpublished — gives the measure of the surprise such a composition must have provoked: "I can see from my window," Delacroix wrote on September 7, 1856, "a parquet layer working in the gallery, bare to the waist. Comparing his color with that of the wall outside, I note that the half-tones of the flesh are so colorful when compared with inert matter [...]. The flesh gains its true color in the open, and most of all in the sun light. A man should only put his head out the window and he is totally different from what he was inside the room; hence, the stupidity of studio studies, which strive at making this color untrue."

Obviously, Caillebotte's early works illustrate a notion of painting and technique supporting the ideas developed by Edmond Duranty in a publication of 1876. Caillebotte found himself in agreement with a text which owed much to Degas. The immediacy and modernity of his work stem from the fact that he seems to have overlooked the questions which agitated his predecessors, pulled as they were between tradition and their ideal of truth and realist observation. This tension was noticeable in Manet's recent paintings: *The Good Pint*, dated 1873, transformed an image that had come from Frans Hals;[12] the following year, Manet responded to Monet's Impressionism by painting *Argenteuil*. Critics reacted before Caillebotte's paintings by trying to invoke references to Dutch paintings. In spite of everything he shared with his friends, however, his art remained remarkably independent. The writer Edmond de Goncourt could not claim his floor-scrapers as he had claimed the washerwomen, the balls at the Opera, and the general spirit of themes he regarded as drawn from his inspiration. Without going too far, it could be said that Caillebotte was able to take into account the most positive aspects of the evolution in the

12. Museum of Fine Arts, Philadelphia.

preceding years in order to assert himself. He was greatly admired for his ability to progress. He could not do this without an overall reflection, a clear intuition of his abilities, and a control of his ideas. His career was built around a

Three Studies for
The Floor-Scrapers, ca 1875
Pencil
18⅞" × 12¼" (48 × 31 cm)
Private collection
Photo Galerie Brame et
Lorenceau, Paris

G. Caillebotta.

consciousness which saved him from the temptation of a moderate realism — many "young" artists like him felt it at one time or another — but it also deprived him of riskier explorations or contradictions.

From the very beginning, his works showed that he had understood the nature of Impressionism. The whole issue of his art is based on this strongly productive understanding, which was also defined and contained by his logical mind.

Caillebotte had met some of the members of the future cooperative named " Société anonyme à capital variable des artistes peintres, sculpteurs, graveurs, etc. " before February 1876, when Renoir and Henri Rouart wrote him a letter inviting him to join them in their next exhibition. He had started to buy their works, especially paintings by Monet, in April. He clearly knew the history of this independent art, " the school of open-air painting ", the " school of the eyes " as it was sometimes described, and he was aware of its multifarious trends and the various difficulties that beset it. The exhibition opening on April 15, 1874, marked the fulfillment of ideas which had had time to come to fruition. The paintings were shown without a screening before a jury nor the aim of winning an award, and the installation took into account the personality of each artist, providing good space and light. Critics reacted positively to the quality of the installation, which contrasted sharply with the enormous accumulation of paintings at the official Salon. The rooms of Nadar's former studio at 35 Boulevard des Capucines created the comfortable atmosphere of a private apartment. Later, Caillebotte was to do everything in his power to maintain and even strengthen this aspect of the show. It would be superfluous to recall here the significance of this first exhibition and the critical reaction. " Let us say that this exhibition is interesting to us because of the light colors, the clearly defined masses, and the quality of impressions, " Philippe Burty wrote. He added, " On second sight, it cannot fail to offend those who have pre-established ideas regarding the finished state of a painting, the *chiaroscuro*, and the choice of attractive sites. " The pictures which were to become famous, pictures by Monet, Renoir, Pissarro, Berthe Morisot, established the optical character of realism — Monet's *Boulevard des Capucines*[13] was called a " kaleidoscope of Parisian life " — the values of movement — a critic noted the " elusive, fleeting, instantaneous quality of movement " — and the unbelievable technique used to achieve this effect: " Come closer, everything vanishes; there remains only an incomprehensible chaos of paint scrapings ".[14] The 1874 exhibition revealed what was at stake artistically, as Caillebotte well realized.

An essential aspect of this new painting needs to be emphasized, however. Like many critics of the time, Caillebotte may have appreciated the diversity in a movement based on the freedom of expression of each artist, and this was confirmed by his choices as a collector. The critic Castagnary voiced the opinion that the " impression " was only a " manner of painting " which would not last long in the face of inevitable future divisions between the stronger artistic temperaments. Before these " rebels " who

13. 1873-1874, William Rockhill Gallery of Atkins Museum of Fine Arts, Kansas City.

14. Ernest Chesneau, «À côté du Salon: II. - Le plein air: Exposition du boulevard des Capucines,» *Paris-Journal*, May 7, 1874.

Sketch, ca 1876
Oil on canvas
10⅜" × 12⅞"
(26.4 × 32.7 cm)
Private collection

were tearing down conventions, another critic, Marc de Montifaud, remarked that " schisms do not happen in the arts " and that a few years would be needed before a certain unity developed from these uneven efforts. The quality of Caillebotte's collection — a part of which is in the collection of the Musée d'Orsay, as we shall see when we examine his bequest in 1894 — stems largely from his awareness of this diversity. His collection was an attempt to record the differences and to capture their historic significance. It was not put together for his own enjoyment only, or in order to satisfy his own aesthetic orientation and provide models for his paintings. Caillebotte did not try to buy the works closest to his own inspiration. He sought to construct the strongest and most representative dimension of a lively and open movement. Better than any words, this collection reveals Caillebotte's particular

Sketch, ca 1876
Oil on wood
4⅞" × 7½ (12.3 × 19 cm)
Private collection

understanding of Impressionism, beyond divisions, and his wish to
capture the vitality of an aesthetic movement.   Notwithstanding
the aspect of " chance " in the purchase of paintings, the result was
a collection of great quality marked by a respect of freedom in the
most productive sense of the word.   Many painters who could
have been featured in the collection were not.   Caillebotte made
a deliberate choice: Degas, Manet, Cézanne, Monet, Renoir, Sisley,
Pissarro.   Then he sought to present the most complete view of
each artist's work, combining his friendship for one or another with
an objective opinion of the paintings.   This is clearly the case with
the seven pastel drawings by Degas, the quality of which is evenly

15. 1875-1876, The Barnes Foundation, Merion, Pennsylvania.

16. 1873-1874, Musée d'Orsay, Paris.

17. Marc de Montifaud, «Exposition du boulevard des Capucines», *L'Artiste*, May 1, 1874.

18. Including *Laundress (Silhouette)*, ca 1874, The Metropolitan Museum of Art, New York. The H.O. Havemeyer Collection.

19. 1873, Musée municipal, Pau.

high, but also with the paintings by Manet: *Angelina* seems to explore even more boldly the unusual effect of the *Balcony*. His choice of paintings by Cézanne highlights the spirit of his collection: *L'Estaque, Farmyard at Auvers, Bathers Resting*,[15] *Vase of Flowers, Country Scene.* This was specially remarkable since Cézanne had provoked Castagnary's comment about " an unbridled romanticism, where nature is merely a pretext for reverie " and he was so far removed from Caillebotte's world, as can be seen from his painting *A Modern Olympia*,[16] " this little naked apparition of pink flesh pushed by a sort of demon into a cloudy empyrean, where a corner of artificial paradise develops like a voluptuous vision. "[17] The selection of pictures by Monet is also significant: *Regatta at Argenteuil*, dated 1872, *Rocks at Belle-Ile, The Luncheon, A Corner in an Apartment, Gare Saint-Lazare*, as well as two other compositions in the same series, entitled *Under the Bridge* and *The Signal*. Renoir was featured with eight striking paintings from his most luminous Impressionist period, including *Woman in the Sun* and *A Ball at the Moulin de la Galette*. Some of the major works by Sisley and mostly Pissarro were representative of the significance of landscape painting. This collection was put together during the period when Caillebotte was at his most productive as a painter and it sheds light both on his personal commitment to the history and daily development of the Impressionist movement and his ability to understand the historic significance of these events. The paintings aroused in him intense feelings which were not due merely to the complex pleasure of ownership. They were feelings related to beliefs of a higher order pushed by a sort of demon into — a life without flourish and a work without eloquence or allegory, whose lucidity aimed at the heart of things.

At the second Impressionist exhibition held in April 1876 at 11 Rue Le Peletier, Caillebotte created a sensation with eight paintings, among them the two versions of the *Floor-Scrapers*. From an unknown painter, he suddenly became a full-fledged Impressionist whose powerful works were the object of discussions. The *Floor-Scrapers* from the collection of the Musée d'Orsay in Paris was to become his most famous painting during his lifetime (see pages 30-31). It fully deserved this honor, serving as it does as an original statement of the most complex values of realism, at a time when Degas was exhibiting his *Washerwomen*[18] and *The Cotton Exchange in New Orleans*.[19] Its theme was so much a part of contemporary experience that nobody could take exception to it. The critic Philippe Burty, a passionate defender of realism, could salute "a faithful

The Floor-Scrapers, 1875
Oil on canvas
39⅝" × 57⅛"
(100.6 × 145 cm)
Musée d'Orsay, Paris
Photo Réunion des
Musées nationaux, Paris

20.   Philippe Burty, «Fine
Art: The Exhibition of the
'Intransigeants'»,
The Academy, London,
April 15, 1876.

21. Émile Zola, «Deux expositions d'art en mai», *Le Messager de l'Europe* [Saint-Petersburg], June 1876. Reprinted in Émile Zola, *Le bon combat de Courbet aux impressionnistes*, an anthology of his writings on art, ed. by Gaëtan Picon, Paris: Savoir/ Hermann, 1974.

representation of life as it expresses itself in the working functions".[20] The following year, he noted that Caillebotte displayed "a curiosity, which is unusual today, about professional types and activities". The painting shows laborers, carpenters skilled in the laying and maintenance of parquet floors, but their work takes place in a bourgeois apartment, a room in the final stages of preparation. The notion of work was captured in a perspective where the work itself would soon be forgotten: Nobody will remember these three workers once the rugs and furniture are installed. The subject seemed trivial and vulgar, but it formed the very basis of the representation. It expressed a capacity for analysis and a consciousness which may have been related to some aspects of contemporary art, and this is the privilege of powerful works. The writer Émile Zola felt disconcerted and did not recognize these floor-scrapers as characters on a level with his own Rougon-Macquart: "Because of its precise rendering, this is anti-artistic painting, neat as glass, bourgeois painting."[21] The precise observation was indeed a significant element: The movements are perfectly attuned to the specific tool used, a plane for the figure on the right, a scraper for the figure in the middle, and a whetting file for the third figure. In the foreground, one can see a file, a hammer, and a bottle of wine and a glass on the marble hearth in front of the fireplace; sacks are lying at the back, forming shapes which have a precise value in the general sparseness of the composition. The latter can be analyzed from a technical and aesthetic point of view. The workers share the space according to a distribution of light that creates an unusual harmony between the figures and the viewer's plunging perspective. The viewer can clearly see the work in progress, whether the work already completed — in full light in the foreground — or the work still to be done on the right side of the picture. The optical reality and the interpretation of effects of perspective provoked negative reactions: The arms were deemed too long or too thin, the bodies were seen as threatening to crash onto the inclining floor, the light came from the back and there were reflections. In fact, these components had all been carefully studied in preparatory drawings of each detail, leading to an oil study which is quite close to the final painting. The group of three carpenters creates a collective rhythm and it also provides a certain social definition of manual labor. Two of the figures seem to be exchanging a few words. The ternary rhythm is repeated in the motif of the paneling. The tonal continuity between the floor and the workers expresses a harmony related to the technical and professional dimension of work. It should be pointed out that Caillebotte eliminated every possible suggestion of an ethical or sentimental interpretation. His laborers owe nothing to classical references. Their truth is entirely contained in what they do. Caillebotte stripped his figures of the poetic humanism characteristic of Jean-François Millet. He depicted with blunt frankness this social borderline between the social reality of working-class labor and aesthetic contemplation. His picture unveils antagonisms or contradictions expressed in the sole confrontation between the vision of an artist who seems to be living in this bourgeois house and that of figures who live in a fundamentally different world. There was another sign of Caillebotte's ambition in this austere work: His signature was painted in the darkest section of the picture and its color matches that of the thin layer of damp wood about to planed off.

Another canvas contributes to the nature of observation in Caillebotte's paintings by introducing the idea of a series. The perspective modifies the intensity in the interpretation as the viewer discovers an older floor-scraper with an assistant, in a room less grand than in the first picture. Another reality comes to the fore, and the knee-pads used by floor-scrapers in their work are more visible. The overall tonality is warmer, the light effects less stark. The disposition of the figures highlights a professional hierarchy between the man who is working with the plane and the other who is sharpening his scraper. A characteristic comment of the period reflects the generally disparaging reaction to such themes. A contemporary critic claimed that the young apprentice was delousing himself, thus deliberately mistaking work for filth, manual work for poverty: "One of these gentlemen has stopped working to devote himself to that kind of little hunt about his body that certain habits of cleanliness would make unnecessary; this could be hardly seen as in good taste."[22] Here again, the parquet floor captures the viewer's attention as a mirror, a motif, and an object. The eye discovers the beauty of an empty space which is made visible and luminous by the very presence of the two workers. Like Degas or Monet, Caillebotte had become an artist who painted that which nobody wished to see and which would not have been seen without him.

Young Man at the Piano also points to Caillebotte's major qualities as an artist (see pages 34-35). Its theme stands in contrast with that of the paintings mentioned above, but the spirit of its composition is similar. Here again, a painting

22. Émile Porcheron, «Promenades d'un flâneur, les impressionnistes», *Le Soleil*, April 4, 1876.

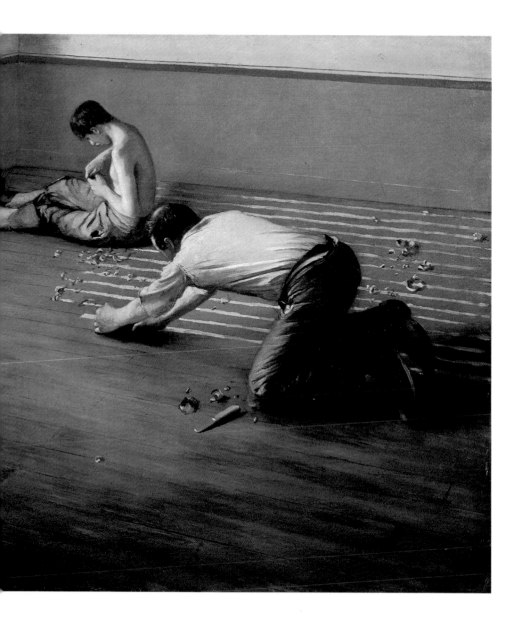

The Floor-Scrapers, 1876
Oil on canvas
31½" × 39⅜" (80 × 100 cm)
Private collection
Photo Giraudon, Vanves

Young Man at the Piano
1876
Oil on canvas
32" × 46" (81.3 × 116.8 cm)
Private collection
Photo Galerie Brame et
Laurenceau, Paris

captures contemporary life both in a general manner and in a revealing moment. The artist's younger brother was the model for the figure of the musician. Martial was then twenty-three years old; he played the piano and composed music. He never had a profession and was to lead the life of a wealthy dilettante, dividing his time between his interest in photography, stamps, gardening and a collection of earthenware. The two brothers were extremely close. Beyond these biographical aspects, the artist knew very well that he was taking up a significant subject in the recent history of realism. His friends had already painted on a similar theme and a whole generation had loved the music of Schumann, Liszt, and Wagner. The composition was prepared with a series of drawings, among them a carefully squared up study of the main figure. The latter is an illustration of both the values of concentration — with its torso cut out in the light — and an intangible moment of music playing. A delicate balance is established between the room, its comfortable furnishings, and the world of music. The perspective construction plays a great role in this remarkable achievement, whereby things do not appear as inert weight but rather combine and create a harmony in which music is only a component. In 1876, critics voiced harsh judgments about the elevated viewpoint, which seemed to upset the balance of the piano, " an Érard seen from a the bird's-eye view" and threatening to crush the musician.[23] The play of light also evoked the tradition of Dutch painters, Vermeer or Pieter de Hooch, a tradition which realist painters claimed openly.

" Is it not a rather pitiful use of his time, colors, and canvas, to devote them to painting the back of a gentleman dressed in a coat of black cloth, bought ready-made at the shop which may or may not be at the corner of the street or the corner of the quay? "[24] The journalist was thus implying that the figure in *Young Man at the Window* shopped in a well-known department store of the time, " Au Coin de Rue " (see page 37). His reaction was fairly typical of the feeling of reality which seized the visitors to the exhibition in the Rue Le Peletier. The viewer sees at the same time the private space of an apartment and the public space of the street but this perception is quite different from the classical experience of a landscape seen from a window. It contains an element of confrontation threatening the balance of values related to that which is inside as opposed to that which is outside. By using his brother René as a model, standing with his back to the room, looking out the window, his hands in his pockets, Caillebotte invented an astonishingly banal

23. *Ibid.*

24. Louis Enault, «Mouvement artistique - L'exposition des Intransigeants dans la galerie Durand-Ruel», *Le Constitutionnel*, April 10, 1876.

and enigmatic character, whose power and consciousness depend only on the function of his eyes. This painting brings to mind some romantic pictures which Caillebotte was unlikely to have known. The comparison with Caspar David Friedrich is informative but only as a demonstration of everything that is canceled out by a realist composition.[25] It also lacks the Goya-like charm of Manet's *Balcony*. The loneliness of this figure is one with the architecture and the whole city. While depicting a window on the third floor of the family's townhouse, facing the Rue the Miromesnil toward the Boulevard Malesherbes, Caillebotte did more than render objective facts. He gave an interpretation of these facts by means of subtle effects, where the light on the balconied fronts of the Haussmann-style buildings, the young trees in the boulevard, and the quiet atmosphere of an elegant district, catches the attention of a man briefly distracted from some occupation. The upholstered and padded armchair plays a major part as a material and social sign of the man's omnipresence. The visible world of the painting and its formal construction can be carefully examined. The viewer believes at first that he sees what the man is seeing from his window but it becomes clearly apparent that this is a naive idea. In fact, the viewer can only see what the man does not see and he can only identify with him by becoming aware of the optical reality of the scene. This is a dissociation and an unattainable objectivity achieved by painting.

The author of the catalogue raisonné of Caillebotte's work, Marie Berhaut, rightly emphasized the connection between his paintings exhibited in 1876 and the text published on this occasion by the writer and critic Edmond Duranty (1833-1880), entitled "The New Painting: Concerning the Group of Artists Exhibiting at the Durand-Ruel Galleries".[26] This is a significant connection because it demonstrates that the ideas articulated by Duranty were developed by the artists themselves, in particular Degas, who was his principal source of inspiration, and also Caillebotte, who played a major part in the emergence of a theory of realism. "The very first idea," Duranty recalled, "was to eliminate the partition separating the artist's studio from everyday life and to introduce the reality of the street that shocks the writer in the "Revue des Deux Mondes."[27] Starting as a rebuttal of Eugène Fromentin's ambivalent opinion in a recent article, "The New Painting" presented itself as a manifesto about a depiction of society and its mores as a whole on the basis of direct observation; it also contained, however, several reminders and warnings. "Farewell to the human body treated like a

Young Man at the Window, 1876
Oil on canvas
45 ¼" × 31 ⅞"
(116.2 × 80.9 cm)
Private collection

25. Kirk Varnedoe, *Gustave Caillebotte*, New Haven, Conn., London: Yale University Press, 1987.

26. Paris: E. Dentu, 1876.

27. *Ibid.*, translated by Charles S. Moffet, in *The New Painting: Impressionism 1874-1886*, exhibition catalogue, The Fine Arts Museums of San Francisco, 1986, p. 44.

vase," Duranty wrote, "with an eye for decoratively curved lines. Farewell to the uniform monotony of the bone structure and the anatomical model beneath the nude. What we need are the special characteristics of a modern person — his clothing, his social setting, at home, or in the street." And he added: "A back should reveal temperament, age, and social position. [...] Hands kept in pockets can be eloquent."[28]

By insisting that truth should penetrate every component of reality, Duranty advocated pictorial means stripped of any eclecticism. He pleaded for a generalized observation in which a figure exists mainly in connection with a specific place and moment in time, whatever its position in society. According to this line of reasoning, even an idle figure acquires a meaning which is equivalent to an act: "And, as we are solidly embracing nature, we will no longer separate a figure from the background of an apartment or a street. In real life a person never appears against empty or vague backgrounds. Instead, surrounding him or behind him are the furniture, fireplaces, curtains, and walls that indicate his financial position, social class, and profession. He will be at a piano, or examining a sample of cotton in an office, or waiting in the wings for the moment to go on stage, or ironing on a makeshift table. He will be having lunch with his family or sitting in his armchair near his worktable, absorbed in thought. He might be avoiding carriages as he crosses the street or glancing at his watch as he hurries across the square. When at rest, he will not be merely pausing or striking a meaningless pose before the photographer's lens. This moment of rest will be as much a part of his life as his actions are."[29] Like Degas or Monet, Caillebotte illustrated this aesthetic approach. His paintings were perceived as the best expression of the different aspects of a reality which are brought to the fore by an unpredictable frame or cropping: "From indoors we communicate with the outside world through windows. A window is yet another frame that is continually with us during the time we spend at home, and that time is considerable. Depending on whether we are near or far, seated or standing, the window frames the scene outside in the most unexpected and varied ways, providing us with constantly changing impromptu views that are the great delights of life."[30]

With the painting *Luncheon*, Caillebotte followed the line of a sort of doctrinaire demonstration by presenting the viewer with an excessive relationship between the figures and the objects. This relationship is particularly evident because the theme of the painting brings to mind earlier works by Courbet,

28. *Ibid.*, pp. 43-44.

29. *Ibid.*, pp. 44-45.

30. *Ibid.*, p. 45.

Luncheon, 1876
Oil on canvas
20 ½" × 29 ½" (52 × 75 cm)
Private collection
Photo Giraudon, Vanves

Renoir, Manet, and Monet, as well as a tradition carried on later by Paul Signac, Pierre Bonnard, Édouard Vuillard, and Henri Matisse. The composition contains a biographical element as a portrait of the artist's mother, a widow since 1874, his brother René, who subsequently died suddenly at the end of the year, and even the artist himself as the plate in the foreground is clearly his. The half-empty glass suggests a presence. The butler Jean Daurelle serves at the table according to established rules. The table is set befittingly for an ordinary luncheon. Nothing indicates a marked luxury but everything hints at a comfortable, well-to-do atmosphere, an elegantly bourgeois dining room as a setting for a moment in time, a meal, and for lives that are separated and isolated in a given space. The harmony created by the black tabletop and the glassware shining in the light imparts a quality of order and quiet austerity to the scene, which the dish of oranges and lemons fails to animate. Nineteenth-century habits are interpreted differently today from what they were in 1876. In those days, the cropping of the image was seen as unusual. Today, we would react more to the family life of these unmarried young men who were having lunch together, perhaps without boredom but also without joy. "This is Impressionism at its worse", a journalist commented, "[...] the table seems at least thirty-six feet long; the frame cuts the plate of one of the three diners in two, and the other two people placed at the far end of the table are so far away that they look absurd."[31]

31. Émile Porcheron, *op. cit.*

Study for
Luncheon, ca 1876
Pencil
18½" × 12¼" (47 × 31 cm)
Private collection
Photo Galerie Brame et
Laurenceau, Paris

Yerres. The Grass in the
Park, Seen From a Lane:
Sunset, Sixth Impression
Before 1879
Oil on canvas
9 ½" × 13" (24 × 33 cm)
Private collection
Photo Galerie Brame et
Lorenceau, Paris

Chapter three

Caillebotte's world: the street and the river

Yerres. The Grass in the
Park, Seen From a Lane:
Sunset, Sixth Impression
Before 1879
Oil on canvas
9½" × 13" (24 × 33 cm)
Private collection
Photo Galerie Brame et
Lorenceau, Paris

32. Musée d'Orsay, Paris.

Caillebotte worked often in the family country home at Yerres, a beautiful house in the classical style with a vast landscape garden, its design and works in the style of eighteenth-century Romanticism.   He stayed there in the summer for long periods at a time.   The river on the edge of the property is a tributary of the Seine, a quiet river suitable for boating and swimming.   This well-kept estate provided themes for many views, which have been catalogued precisely, as well as landscapes of the surrounding countryside.   Some views are merely studies indicating that the young Caillebotte was working constantly but they also show that he had a taste for unusual themes.

The painting called *The Yerres, Rain* or *River Bank in the Rain* (see page 48) is remarkable because of its foreground bordered by an embankment, which cuts through the composition, the surface of the water, with reflections and rippling pools creating a sort of rhythm, and a background that carries the eyes much further.   The colors are both severe and subtle, totally unconventional. The brushstrokes seem to glide on a opaque mirror.   Rain drops appear to make waves depicted by the artist with childish innocence.   The ripples may also be caused by bubbles rising from the bottom of the river and they suggest a material life which becomes the artist's main motif and highlights its singularity.

A group portrait in the open, *Portraits in the Country*, takes one back to the company of the ladies of the house, evoking the quiet and protective world in the shade of which Caillebotte was experimenting with his new vision (see pages 46-47).   This afternoon gathering by the corner of the house, near the orange trees in their boxes, reflects an intensely real everyday experience in the life of the artist.   His cousin Marie Caillebotte is in the foreground, in a summer dress; her mother is sitting on a bench, facing a family friend.   In the background Madame Caillebotte is reading, with her embroidery frame in front of her.   She made beautiful embroidery and seemed to have communicated this passion to the rest of her family.   Her son Gustave is supposed to have created designs for her.   Here, he depicted the most traditional habits of his time.   He must have known Fantin-Latour's paintings on this theme and derived a special pleasure from rendering his models working in the open at their delicate craft, creating a perspective construction powerfully structured by outlines and colors.   The difference between this painting and Bazille's *Family Reunion*[32] dated 1867 is significant: Caillebotte did not need to be recognized as a painter.   He was accepted by a group that never felt uneasy under the scrutiny of an outsider.   In his youth, in 1853, Bonnat

Portraits in the Country
1876
Oil on canvas
37⅜" × 43¾" (95 × 111 cm)
Musée Baron Gérard,
Bayeux
Gift of Mr. and
Mrs. Chaplain, in Memory
of Mrs. Fermal
née Zoé Caillebotte

33. *Portrait of the Artist's Mother, Brother, and Sister*, 1853, Musée Bonnat, Bayonne.

34. Jacques [pseud.], «Menus propos», *L'Homme libre*, April 12, 1877.

35. Philippe Burty, «L'Exposition des impressionnistes», *La République française*, April 25, 1877.

The River Yerres, Rain or River Bank in the Rain
1875
Oil on canvas
31⅛" × 23¼" (81 × 59 cm)
Indiana University
Art Museum
Bloomington
Gift of Mrs. N.H. Noyes

had also painted a family portrait inspired by the tradition of Dutch painting, which was greatly admired by the realist painters.[33] Caillebotte's painting was fairly well received at the Impressionist exhibition of 1877: " A whole family, mother, daughter, grandmother, friend, sewing or embroidering near a white villa, the half-open windows of which send out puffs of bourgeois fragrance ", a critic wrote.[34]

Like Manet, but without the feeling of closeness that existed between the painter of *Olympia* and his mother, Caillebotte painted a portrait of his mother when she was fifty years old and nearing the end of her life (see pages 50-51). Her needlework required her whole attention, leading to an effect of absence, a face without eyes. " An intelligent study, tight, with feeling ", Burty commented.[35] The gilt decorations, the lace, the curtains, and the black dress created a harmony in which Caillebotte's talent as a colorist could shine.

The third Impressionist exhibition owes its success in large part to Caillebotte's efforts to persuade the others to pursue the path previously set. A note addressed to Pissarro shows that he was still hoping that Manet would join the group. He worked unsparingly and must have overcome many hesitations when he rented at his own expense a large apartment on the third floor at 6 Rue Le Peletier, on the corner of the Boulevard Haussmann. The elegance of the large bourgeois rooms and the quality of the installation brought a great number of visitors. We have a fairly precise description of the installation in the articles published in the journal of Georges Rivière, " L'Impressionniste, Journal d'Art ". Newspapers featured many critical reviews and caricatures. The play by Ludovic Halévy, " The Cicada ", performed in October at the Théâtre des Variétés, indicated how popular this new painting had become. Caillebotte was showing six pictures with seventeen other participants to the exhibition, including Cézanne, Degas, Armand Guillaumin, Franc Lamy, Alphonse Mureau, Monet, Berthe Morisot, Pissarro, Renoir, and Sisley.

The Pont de l'Europe is a long bridge which was completed in 1868 and spans the yards of the Saint-Lazare train station; its iron structure, design, and function made it one of the most remarkable achievements of the Second Empire. With its squares, its X-shaped plan leading to wide modern streets and Haussmann-style buildings, it stood as a successful illustration of the adaptation, by means of urban planning, of the city to its function as a capital. Exhibited at the Salon of 1874, Manet's *Gare Saint-Lazare* had already evoked a viewpoint on the bridge

Madame Martial
Caillebotte
Mother of the Artist, 1877
Oil on canvas
32¼" × 28¼" (83 × 72 cm)
Private collection
Photo Giraudon, Vanves

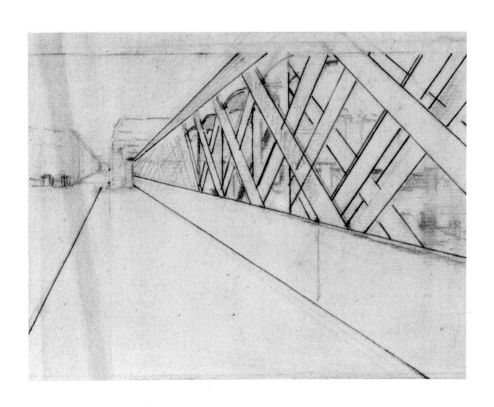

Study for
Pont de l'Europe, ca 1876
Pencil, 6 ¼" × 7 ½"
(16 × 19 cm)
Private collection
Photo Galerie Brame et
Lorenceau, Paris

Study for
Pont de l'Europe
The Iron Girders, 1876
Oil on canvas
22" × 18" (55.5 × 45.7 cm)
Private collection
Photo Giraudon, Vanves

Sketch for
Pont de l'Europe, 1876
Oil on canvas
12⅝" × 18⅛" (32 × 46 cm)
Musée des Beaux-Arts
Rennes
Photo Louis Deschamps

as a expression of the poetry of contemporary life.[36] In 1877 Monet showed a series of views of the Saint-Lazare train station which are still regarded as among his most powerful works.[37] Caillebotte lived in the neighborhood and he took up a theme he knew very well. His painting, *Pont de l'Europe*, aimed at fulfilling an ambition he shared with his friends. In his pamphlet, Duranty had ranked the railways as the setting most suitable for unusual and almost endless possibilities in the " cropping " of an image. The bold composition of the painting highlights the beauty of a construction which modifies the traditional elements of a perspective view. The artist's perception of the very nature of the iron bridge brings to the fore its dynamic power within the urban space. The bridge is a

36. The National Gallery of Art, Washington, D.C.

Pont de l'Europe, 1876
Oil on canvas
49 ¼" × 70 ⅞"
(125 × 180 cm)
Musée du Petit Palais
Geneva

37.   Caillebotte was to
own three paintings from
this series, one now at the
Musée d'Orsay, and two
which were not accepted
as part of his bequest,
*Gare Saint-Lazare,
Outside View, Sketch
(Under the Bridge)* and
*Gare Saint-Lazare, The
Signal.*

Studies for
Pont de l'Europe, ca 1876
Pencil, 18⅞" × 12¼"
(48 × 31 cm)
Private collection
Photo Galerie Brame et
Lorenceau, Paris

pretext for an outing of both elegant passers-by and shuffling
workers. It creates a delicately pale light that unveils the
diversity of a moving world. Caillebotte proceeded
methodically, with a series of drawings and oil studies, seeking a
complex balance between optical facts and their
interpretation. The landscape would be almost unpleasant
without the figures. The main figure is a man, generally seen
as representing the artist himself, " chatting intimately with a
very pretty woman ". " Our compliments, Monsieur
Caillebotte ", a critic exclaimed.[38] This element of elegance and
observation takes its full value from the fact that it is cleverly
placed at a distance from the viewer, notwithstanding the

38. Anon., «L'Exposition
des impressionnistes»,
Le Temps, April 7, 1877.

reaction of the critics who gave it pride of place. In fact, the formal and material components of the whole composition require that space and time be indicated before any fragment of narration. A dog enters the field of vision, creating an element of movement, consistency, and surprise as a true part of society without which a sidewalk would not be what it is. The worker in a smock occupies a significant position in the foreground, at the point of intersection of the railing and the girder trellis. He is watching the comings and goings of the engines below and stands effectively for the differences in values related to differences in social positions. Caillebotte records this obvious fact because the bridge is also the best setting for this contrast

Studies for
Pont de l'Europe, ca 1876
Pencil, 18½" × 12¼"
(47 × 31 cm)
Private collection
Photo Galerie Brame et
Lorenceau, Paris

Pont de l'Europe
1876-1880
Oil on canvas
41 ½" × 51 ⅛"
(105.3 × 129.9 cm)
Kimbell Art Museum
Fort Worth, Texas
Photo Michael Bodycomb

between bourgeois and working-class worlds. The picture's detailed precision may bring to mind a misleading analogy with photography but the harmonious effects of light create a freedom of vision which accounts for the power of the composition. The urban landscape becomes a setting for a freedom that turns a passer-by into an artist, an urban laborer into a stroller in idle contemplation, a dog into a habitué of the neighborhood, and combines steel engineering with steam expanding into the atmosphere, the industrial world with the most delicate feelings of life, the comings and goings of individuals in varying degrees of isolation with a contemporary society in its recent experience of democracy.

The version now in the collection of the Kimbell Art Museum in Fort Worth is interesting from a different point of view. It was probably made after the one above, and it is not a partial study. It is a variant version, complete in its own right, painted in an astonishing bluish-gray monochrome. It takes up the act of seeing as a theme, which is rendered by means of the standing figure looking out and the material structure of the bridge which makes it possible to look out. In its extreme fragmentation, the architecture of the bridge hints at the existence of a consistent world entirely related to industrial and technical modernization. The elegant man's halt evokes the anonymous dress and looks of a contemporary bourgeois, as well as the possible modular repetition of such a theme. The asymmetrical positioning of the figures, combined with the symmetrical design of the girder trellis, suggests a movement which brings the composition together and provokes an intellectual reaction related to the colors. By cutting off the lower section of the painting at the level of the legs, Caillebotte emphasized the effect of pure contemplation and drew a powerful effect from the confrontation between a man's profile and the intersection of metal structures. The complex cropping of the landscape brings to mind a multiplicity of possible motifs, among which the standing figure is not the most important any more.

Because of its size (83½" × 108¾"), theme, and realist intensity, *Paris Street, Rainy Day* was Caillebotte's masterpiece (see pages 60-61). The picture is a true reflection of his personality as an artist and it possesses a particular presence and quality which turned it into a legendary image. It depicts a moment in the present, but also a moment in reality which seems to relate to both past and present, as Baudelaire advocated in " Le Peintre de la vie moderne ". This painting, however, is very remote from Baudelaire's world. A better parallel would be Manet's painting

Paris Street, Rainy Day
1877
Oil on canvas
83½" × 108¼"
(212.2 × 276.2 cm)
The Art Institute, Chicago
Charles H. and
Mary F.S. Worcester Fund

Nana, dated the same year, which was rejected by the Salon.[39] The man with a hat passing before us seems to belong to the same world as Nana's, despite the fact that he stands here for the respectability of contemporary bourgeois couples. This obvious representation of social values makes *Paris Street* very different from urban landscapes painted at the same date by De Nittis, Béraud, Degas, Maureau, and Ludovic Piette. Caillebotte would produce more anecdotal views of Paris but this painting is much more ambitious. The near life-size figures bring to mind a surprising relationship with history paintings and impart a hitherto unknown dimension to common objects. Philippe Burty, for instance, noted that the composition called for "the rendering of umbrellas as large as life".[40] Much has been made of the umbrellas that all seem to be "taken from the racks of the Louvre and Bon Marché department stores".[41] So many umbrellas, to each one his own, and so little rain. One could not see the downpour, only a damp atmosphere, a shiny mist, and this seemed surprising. Caillebotte's title gave the answer: rainy day, as if he had tried to eliminate the narrative event of a downpour. Even rain had become the sign of daily and absolute uniformity.

Duranty had evoked an analogy with photography. It was, however, only an analogy: "This gives us an idea of what photography will be when the means will have been found to reproduce the intensity and delicacy of colors".[42] The painterly precision in *Paris Street* also recalled the Dutch masters: "It is a spacious intersection, with its sidewalks and cobblestones washed by the waters from the sky, like the old bricks of Amsterdam by the Dutch housewives".[43] Caillebotte had proceeded methodically, starting with a ruled perspective construction and including detailed studies of the main and secondary figures. The oil studies capture in a remarkable manner this split approach which was to be combined in the final composition. But, like one of the partial studies for *Pont de l'Europe*, the study of cobblestones acquires an individual presence by which a void can be expressed. Duranty wrote about "the language of an empty apartment", and he complained that "almost all landscape artists lack a feel for the structure of the ground". He must have been more than satisfied with *Paris Street* since the cobblestones become a lively part of the composition, constructive elements which are meant to be seen, closely examined, and admired. After Watteau, Caillebotte's methodical genius made the cobblestones enter history, and one may wonder what the painting would be like

39. 1877, Kunsthalle, Hamburg.

40. Philippe Burty, *op. cit.*

41. E. Lepelletier, «Les Impressionnistes», *Le Radical*, April 8, 1877.

42. Edmond Duranty, *op. cit.*

43. E. Lepelletier, *op. cit.*

44. *Ibid.*

without them. "You can count them, measure them, study them as a geologist, as a chemist, as a surveyor and as a paver."[44] A whole political and social history is depicted by the lamppost, the granite slabs of the sidewalk, and the Haussmann-style façades of the buildings. Urban dwellers are walking freely at the crossings of the Rue de Saint-Pétersbourg, Rue de Moscou, and Rue de Turin, whereby they demonstrate the very function of this star-shaped intersection. The feeling of expansive space is emphasized by the perspective view of the streets at eye level with the main figures.

The whole composition lends itself to a detailed analysis showing the significance of harmonic relationships for the general balance of the figures. Rational methodology and image become one, resulting in a strange awareness of both the rules of spatial construction and of its expressive power. In 1884 Seurat was to explore the same relationship, but starting from different premises, when he painted *Sunday Afternoon on the Island of Grande-Jatte*. He transformed Caillebotte's bourgeois couple into a more ironic and ambiguous image, but

Study for
Paris Street, Rainy Day
Cobble Stones, 1877
Oil on canvas
12⅝" × 15¾" (32 × 40 cm)
Private collection
Photo Galerie Brame et
Lorenceau, Paris

Study for Paris Street
Rainy Day
1877
Pencil, 18½" × 12¼"
(47 × 31 cm)
Private collection
Photo Galerie Brame et
Lorenceau, Paris

this would be less apparent were it not for the evidence achieved in *Rue de Paris*. Indeed, Caillebotte's figures in the foreground seem so natural that one must make an effort to perceive their originality. Nowhere can we find the equivalent rendering of daily banality.

It would be misleading to propose a narrative and psychological interpretation of this couple. One can see nothing but a gentleman and a lady passing by, a young, elegant and bourgeois couple whose attention is attracted by something which we cannot see. This "nothing" replaces individual inner life with appearances and social self, and it fills the painting. Like the cobblestones, Caillebotte's figures have their place and play a part without which there would be an

irreparable gap in the painting.   It is a strange achievement to
be able to consider a distance with such intensity for that which
would seem to exclude any distance.

The notion that Caillebotte worked within a scheme taking
the street as a motif imparts more significance to his *House
Painters* (see pages 66-67).   The social observation noted in
the paintings above is aimed here at the work of urban
laborers.   The gray weather and its subdued light produce a
different atmosphere but it remains in keeping with Caillebotte's
characteristic harmony.   The street is a typically straight street
of the Paris designed by Baron Haussmann, treeless, its sidewalks

Study for
The House Painters
Ca 1877
Pencil, 18½" × 12¼"
(47 × 31 cm)
Private collection
Photo Galerie Brame et
Lorenceau, Paris

Study for
The House Painters
Ca 1877
Pencil, 18⅞" × 12¼"
(48 × 31 cm)
Private collection
Photo Galerie Brame et
Lorenceau, Paris

The House Painters
1877
Oil on canvas
35⅛" × 45¾"
(89.2 × 116.2 cm)
Private collection
Photo Giraudon, Vanves

made of slabs of granite. The decoration of the outside of a restaurant evoke the years of work for the transformation of the urban landscape. Despite this opening, which creates a bold connection between the street, the sidewalk, and the sky, the house painters capture the viewer's attention and lead it toward the restaurant window. The double ladders were the object of several preparatory drawings and they fill the space very effectively. One can guess that the painter in a straw hat is specialized in sign writing, while his companion with a cap, who is assessing the work in progress, may be the master or the foreman. Their respective postures reflect a social reality. Caillebotte does not depict the city as a picturesque setting animated by painters at work, but as a world entirely organized around economic activities, activities of individuals with technical skills. The viewer has a glimpse at different objects, the glass window, the curtains, the wine bottles, each seeming to imply that a similar social reality exists everywhere and that it would be a lie or moral blindness to ignore this reality.

Man With Bucket of Paint
Study for
The House Painters
Ca 1877
Pencil, 18⅝" × 12⅛"
(47 × 30.7 cm)
Private collection
Photo Galerie Brame et
Lorenceau, Paris

Study for
The House Painters
Ca 1877
Pencil
Private collection
Photo Galerie Brame et
Lorenceau, Paris

Rooftops in the Snow,
1878
Oil on canvas
25⅝" × 31⅞" (65 × 81 cm)
Musée d'Orsay, Paris
Photo Réunion des
Musées nationaux, Paris

Chapter four

Optical illusions as such

The 1877 exhibition was a short-lived success. The economic recession deeply affected the artists who could rely only on a small group of patrons, such as Chocquet, Murer, and Hoschedé (who was declared bankrupt in August 1877), or on their mutual assistance. The organization of the World Fair in 1878 added to their difficulties, as it attracted the attention of a wide public whose general attitude toward their works was still hostile. For these reasons an exhibition could not be put together in 1878, despite Caillebotte's efforts. Cézanne, Sisley, and Renoir decided to submit paintings to the official Salon of 1879. Berthe Morisot also withdrew because she was expecting a child. All of Caillebotte's talents as a negotiator and organizer were necessary for a fourth exhibition to take place at No. 28 Avenue de l'Opéra from April 10 to May 11, 1879. Fifteen artists were featured: Félix Bracquemond and Marie Bracquemond, Caillebotte, Adolphe-Félix Cals, Mary Cassatt, Degas, Louis Forain, Albert Lebourg, Monet, Pissarro, Piette (who had died recently), Rouart, Henry Somm, Charles Tillot, and Federico Zandomeneghi. Degas had brought his friends into the group who, by that time, called itself a "group of independent artists" rather than "Impressionists".

This was not just a matter of semantics but it reflected the group's inner conflicts regarding the real benefits derived from the artistic independence it claimed in 1874. The artists' defections were made up for by the number of works exhibited: twenty-five paintings by Caillebotte, thirty-eight by Pissarro, twenty-nine by Monet, twenty-five by Degas. Caillebotte had lent several pictures from his private collection, he had assembled and luxuriously framed the works, he had sent out the necessary letters, and he had even worked on the final installation. He worried about the results of such efforts and took responsibility for the doubts of his friends who were less well-off than he was. His letter to Monet dated April 10 was addressed to an anxious and rather skeptical friend: " We are saved. By five o'clock this afternoon receipts were more than four hundred francs. Two years ago on the opening day, which is the worst, we had less than three hundred and fifty [...]. Don't think, for instance, that Degas has sent the twenty-five or thirty pictures he was supposed to send. This morning there were eight paintings by him. He is very trying, but we have to admit that he has great talent. " Toward the end of the exhibition, on May 1st, he was able to express relief: " Receipts are still increasing. Today, we have about ten thousand five hundred francs. " The results were good: There were about 15,400 visitors and each participating artist received 439 francs. Mary Cassatt used this sum to buy two pictures, one by Monet, the other by Degas. Caillebotte's great private wealth put a singular slant on these financial matters but he could feel that Monet kept at a distance because of doubts: " Manet himself is starting to see that he chose the wrong way. Cheer up! " In fact Monet decided to exhibit at the Salon the following year, as he hoped to sell paintings to the dealer Georges Petit.[45] Therefore, Caillebotte needed to deploy his efforts on three fronts. He had to make a statement by other means than his paintings alone and struggle to reconcile people whose interests diverged.

The paintings he showed at the fourth exhibition created a sensation. Caillebotte was given pride of place in Draner's caricatures for "Charivari". It was said over and again that he was very wealthy and he was regarded as a new leader of the Impressionist group, a new Manet, at a time when the latter seemed on the verge of official acceptance and his paintings *In the Conservatory*[46] and *Boating*[47] were hanging at the Salon. Caillebotte presented a wide choice of works, boating scenes, portraits, decorative panels, and pastels; he even showed a calf or a young cow that aroused much comment. Never before had the use of color seemed so outlandish. "These triumphant daubings clamor the *Ça ira* of the new school [a song from the French Revolution] as loudly as possible," wrote Louis Leroy, who for years had been making capital of the many episodes in this artistic revolution.[48] Caillebotte's youth, however, his energy and independent spirit earned him the praise of critics who appreciated in him an artist who renewed his inspiration year after year.

His pictures of boating parties presented a sport without the ambiguity which paintings by Renoir, Monet, and Manet evoked with such obvious pleasure. Caillebotte's young men rowing or

45. Letter to Théodore Duret, dated March 8, 1880, in Daniel Wildenstein, *Claude Monet, Biographie et catalogue raisonné*, vol. 1, Lausanne and Paris, 1974, p. 438, letter 173.

46. 1879, Nationalgalerie, Staatliche Museen Preussicher Kulturbesitz, Berlin.

47. 1874, The
Metropolitan Museum
of Art, New York.
H.O. Havemeyer
Collection.

48. Louis Leroy, «Beaux-
Arts», *Charivari*,
April 17, 1879.

Oarsmen
on the River Yerres, 1877
Oil on canvas
31⅞" × 45⅝"
(81 × 116 cm)
Private collection
Photo Giraudon, Vanves

canoeing are not seeking some romantic encounters. They are having fun like well-behaved boys. *Oarsmen on the River Yerres* makes us aware of the effort of two rowers pulling together in time (see pages 72-73). Their clothes indicate that they practice this fashionable sport regularly and seriously, but the fact that the figure in the foreground should smoke a pipe adds an element of familiarity. Instead of a face, the viewer can only see a straw hat and two arms, but Caillebotte clearly knew this man. He may have been seeking some sort of pleasure but only if he could share it with one of his peers, as a member of a sort of club where he did not need a face.

Oarsman in a Top Hat provides a sharp contrast. This rower is a distinguished young man, pulling at the oars in street clothes, as if he had only come for a few hours of leisure. His eyes are exactly level with the banks of the river. The entire composition focuses on a portrait expressing a rhythm of life, a certain remoteness, feelings imparting a genuine consistency to the figure. He has in him the makings of a character from a novel, bringing to mind novels by Henry James or Guy de Maupassant, or films by Luchino Visconti. Caillebotte had captured a contemporary face whose loneliness expressed one of the most significant dimension of the nineteenth century.

He achieved other surprising effects with the motif of a flat-bottomed skiff. He clearly loved paddling in a small flotilla of canoes gliding easily over the green waters of the river Yerres (see page 76). It was the inspiration for several compositions marked by the humor characteristic of a wide family gathering of well-bred people on holiday.

Caillebotte did not display the irony of a Seurat or the Nabi group but he carefully recorded an adult world at play whose image in the landscape was somewhat removed from reality. Their games seemed to create toys which did not carry the imagination. Their skiffs were not floating down any exotic river, their light paddles were not striking the water to the rhythm of a search for yet undiscovered lands. Nature was colonized by leisure activities but this very nature resembled a picture in a park. Caillebotte depicted this with great sharpness without drawing any conclusions.

The fifth exhibition of "Independent Artists" was held at No. 10 Rue des Pyramides during April 1880. Eighteen artists took part but Gauguin's arrival in the group did not make up for Monet's absence. Monet declared shortly afterward: "The little clique has become a great club which opens its doors to the

Oarsman in a Top Hat
1877
Oil on canvas
35½" × 46⅛" (90 × 117 cm)
Private collection
Photo Giraudon, Vanves

Skiffs, 1878
Oil on canvas
61 ¹³⁄₁₆" × 44 ½"
(157 × 113 cm)
Musée des Beaux-Arts
Rennes
Photo Louis Deschamps

Bather Preparing to Dive
Ca 1878
Oil on canvas
45 ½" × 35"
(117 × 89 cm)
Private collection
Photo Christie's, London

A Man Docking His Skiff
1878
Oil on canvas
29" × 36½" (73.6 × 92.7 cm)
Virginia Museum of
Fine Arts, Richmond
Collection
Mr. and Mrs. Paul Mellon

first-come dauber".[49] Critics in general noted a slackening in the quality and a lack of unity highlighted by the presence of numerous paintings by Jean-François Raffaëlli. Caillebotte was featured with a few members of the original group — Degas, Guillaumin, Berthe Morisot, Pissarro, and Rouart — but too many second-rate artists made the show less interesting and visitors were fewer. In one of his articles entitled "Naturalism at the Salon", Émile Zola made a rather discouraging assessment and aimed his criticism at the heart of the collective project: "It is a great pity that not one artist in this group should have achieved a powerful and definite expression of this new formula, elements of which are scattered in all their respective works. The formula is there, infinitely divided. Nowhere, in any of their works, does it seem to have been used by a master. They are all forerunners. The man of genius is not yet born."[50] This was a very unfair judgment on the part of a man yielding such authority. In this context, the differences between Caillebotte and Degas seemed to be due to minor matters but they reflected in reality deeply divergent opinions.

Although Caillebotte's paintings do not contain a narrative line, his naturalism and its possible echo in contemporary literature are particularly evident in the two interior scenes exhibited in 1880. They do not have the somewhat suffocating atmosphere of the scenes evoking the family apartment in the Rue de Miromesnil. Caillebotte was by now living with his brother Martial at No. 31 Boulevard Haussmann, behind the Opera, in a neighborhood he was to depict from his balcony. More than ever, his paintings reflect to the specific viewpoint of a wealthy bourgeois. The theme of his paintings, however, suggests a familiarity with a life and domesticity which were not entirely his. He depicted a couple in a relationship marked by habits and tranquility.

The two paintings play off one another (see pages 80-81 and 82). The smaller of the two appears to reverse roles: The man, who is always regarded as the husband, is reading some novel while lying on a sofa. He seems minuscule among huge pillows. In the foreground, his wife is also reading: not a newspaper — this would be too much — but some journal or magazine. The writer and critic Joris-Karl Huysmans, who was singularly apt to understand this unusual relationship, salutes this painting as a celebration of the most trivial aspect of married life. This lady, he explains, does not wear the makeup of an actress or even worse. She just brushed her skin with a

49. E. Taboureux, «Claude Monet», *La Vie Moderne*, June 12, 1880, 380, 25, quoted in John Rewald, *The History of Impressionism*, New York: Museum of Modern Art, 1961, p. 447.

50. Émile Zola, «Le Naturalisme au Salon», (4 articles), *Le Voltaire*, June 18-22, 1880.

Interior
Woman Reading, 1880
Oil on canvas
25⅝" × 31⅞" (65 × 81 cm)
Private collection
Photo Giraudon, Vanves

51. Joris-Karl Huysmans, «L'Exposition des Indépendants en 1880», *L'Art moderne*, Paris: G. Charpentier, 1883.

52. Eugène Véron, «Cinquième exposition des Indépendants», *L'Art*, 1880.

"bismuth powder, tinted rose for blonds, or in Rachel tone for brunettes".[51] At the time, Caillebotte's exact observation, which brings to mind Degas's pitiless eye, was regarded as excessive: "Viewers laughed a lot at Monsieur Caillebotte's little husband".[52]

The other painting, which is larger, also presents this ordinary domesticity but in a comfortable apartment. Huysmans called it a masterpiece. He could recognize the life of Parisians "in an apartment facing the street, its light subdued by the hangings on the windows and softened by the muslin of the little curtains." He noted "the big gilt letterings of commercial signs creeping along the front of balcony railings". This was a major motif in realist art, whether in painting or in literature, but Caillebotte used it in an original manner, cropping the letters, which became difficult to reconstruct or even pronounce. The scene evokes the neighborhood around the Opera, a financial and commercial district. The couple seems well-off without excess: "This is a moment of contemporary life, fixed just as it is". This celebrated "just as it is" was achieved through the effective positioning of the female figure, her back to the room, filling the window frame. A symmetrical figure is vaguely outlined at the window across the street. Huysmans felt the very pulse of life in this idle scene and its "whiff of domesticity". He believed he could actually see, hear, and touch: "The woman who looks idly at the street is quivering, palpitating; one can see the small of her back moving under the marvelous dark velvet of her dress; if you touch her with your finger, she will yawn, turn around, and exchange some pointless words with a husband who is hardly interested by some incident in the newspaper."

Caillebotte painted many portraits. His more significant works may display a special anonymous quality but he also produced works illustrating the notion of portraits as such. The pastel dated 1878, *Portrait of Madame X*, presents a rare and interesting confrontation of two people staring at the viewer: the female model in street clothes posing in an armchair and a portrait, within a portrait, of a man posing in an interior (see page 84-85). The resulting unusual effect is heightened by a harmony of blue and gold tones and the general staging of the composition, as the man's portrait on an easel is drawn in Caillebotte's characteristic style. The viewer is facing these two gazes and he expects an explanation which is not to be found in the composition, as if every confrontation between the image of a woman and that of a man required an explanation.

Interior
Woman at the Window, 1880
Oil on canvas
45¾" × 35" (116 × 89 cm)
Private collection
Photo Giraudon, Vanves

Portrait of Madame X,
1878
Pastel, 24 $^{13}/_{16}$" × 19 $^{11}/_{16}$"
(63 × 50 cm)
Musée Fabre, Montpellier
Photo Frédéric Jaulmes
Montpellier

Optical illusions as such

53. 1876, Musée d'Orsay, Paris.

54. 1881-1882, Courtauld Institute Galleries, London.

55. 1868, Bayerische Staatsgemäldesammlungen, Neue Pinakothek, Munich.

56. Joris-Karl Huysmans, *op.cit.*, pp. 96-97.

In a Café deals with a theme often treated by Degas (for instance his painting entitled *The Absinthe Drinkers*[53]) and Manet, who painted several pictures around his café Reichshoffen and subsequently exhibited *A Bar at the Folies-Bergère*[54] in 1882 with critical acclaim. Caillebotte was interested in the motif of a mirror and he had already explored the reflected image in his *Self-Portrait at the Easel*. The mirror did not break the logic in the composition, it even strengthened the constructive element in the act of looking. The viewer notes, for instance, that the coat is hanging in the middle of the picture, that the top of the table is placed at an equal distance from the top of the bench and the bottom of the painting. This geometry reinforces the dynamic power of perception. The figure may bring to mind that of Manet's *Lunch in the Studio*[55] but he is staring at two card players, whom we can see in the mirror. One must look at the painting closely to see that a terrace protected by a canvas awning is reflected in another mirror behind the players. The painting concentrates a whole virtual space which expands on either side of the canvas, as indicated by the benches. Huysmans immediately noted the accuracy of Caillebotte's observation. He perceived the banality of a big café in a decor which, today, would not appear so mediocre, and he started raving at this pint of "mediocre beer", which he recognized by "its soapy head". He also saw "a bench of purplish velvet which was turning the color of wine lees from the wear due to the continual rubbing of the backs of customers, [...] a big mirror with a gold frame, speckled with fly-spots". He understood about the players: "They are people sitting at a table to forget the bother of the circumstances that make them a living, they think no great thoughts and play quite simply to be distracted from the dreariness of bachelorhood or marriage." He described the main figure standing in the foreground as belonging to a world where everything can be seen, as in a theater where everybody holds a part: "And this barfly, with his hat pushed back onto the nape of his neck, his hands firmly in his pockets, we have seen him in every beer hall, calling the waiters by their first names, chatting and joking about backgammon and billiards, smoking and spitting, filling himself with beers on credit."[56]

At the beginning of May 1881, Caillebotte wrote a long letter to Camille Pissarro, who was closely associated with the fate of the Impressionist exhibitions. This interesting letter lists his main complaints against Degas, whom he perceived as responsible for a disarray which Caillebotte believed could be

In a Café, 1880
Oil on canvas
61" × 45 ¼" (155 × 115 cm)
Musée des Beaux-Arts, Rouen
Photo Dagli Orti, Paris

still overcome. Despite its measured tone, it shows the distance between the two men, Degas and Caillebotte. They were so different in character albeit close in artistic inspiration, culture, and background and they had just discovered their difference, which may have been due to more than their character. The letter expresses also the strength of Caillebotte's ideals and their limitations, as they were suddenly brought to light. He believed in a collective purpose based on purely artistic grounds: "What is to become of our exhibitions? My firm opinion is the following: We ought to continue, and continue only in an artistic direction. All things considered, this is the sole direction of any interest to us all. I am asking, therefore, that an exhibition be organized with all the artists who have shown real interest in this matter, that is you, Monet, Renoir, Sisley, Madame Morisot, Mademoiselle Cassatt, Cézanne, and Guillaumin; Gauguin if you wish, perhaps Cordey, and myself. And that's all since Degas refuses to participate in a show on such a basis."[57] Then he drew a long list of charges against Degas: "Degas brought disarray among us." He accused him of spending more time talking at the Café de la Nouvelle Athènes or in elegant society than actually working. He reproached him for invoking reasons for himself which he denied others: "Today he claims to have financial needs which he did not accept in the case of Monet and Renoir." He also reproached him for Raffaëlli's participation in the show: "He claims that he wanted to have Raffaëlli and the others because Monet and Renoir had backed out and there had to be someone. But for three years he has been pestering Raffaëlli to join us, long before the defection of Monet, Renoir, and even Sisley." He made him responsible for bringing in such artists as Ludovic Lepic, Alphonse Legros, and Alphonse Maureau: "What a combat unit in the great cause of Realism!!!" He then turned to Pissarro, to whom he granted a sort of moral right because he had never weakened, and he clearly asked him to separate himself from Degas in order to recreate a unity: "I am asking you: Don't we have a duty to support one another and forgive our respective weaknesses rather than destroy one another? [...] Had there been only one issue between us, that of art, we would have always agreed. It was Degas who put the matter on another level and it would be very foolish to suffer from the results of his madness."

Clearly, Caillebotte wished to recreate the group of independent artists and, by forcing a break between Degas and his friends, to put on an exhibition in 1881. Pissarro felt embarrassed. Without getting involved in the details of the

57. Letter to Pissarro, January 24, 1881, in Marie Berhaut, *Caillebotte, sa vie, son œuvre*, Paris, 1978, pp. 245-246, letter 22.

problem, he doubted whether the issue could be resolved in purely artistic terms. He could even foresee additional problems. His own sense of loyalty made it seem unfair to dismiss some artists in order to bring back others, who had left the group, and to abide by their conditions. Finally, he reminded Caillebotte that Degas had been sometimes lucky in his recruits, if only when he had invited him to show with the group. Caillebotte was firmly decided not to repeat the experience of the previous year and he did not take part in the show of 1881.

Study of a Man Sitting
Study for
The Bezique Game, ca 1880
Pencil, 18½" × 11⅞"
(47 × 30 cm)
Private collection
Photo Galerie Brame et
Lorenceau, Paris

Chapter five

The vision of things: the city and the display of goods

In January 1881, Pissarro had wisely warned Caillebotte against excessive optimism and confidence: "One day, you may see that I was right, when you see the shaky ground of the arts collapse under you."[58] The lesson of the 1881 exhibition was useful and Caillebotte's viewpoint prevailed in the end. He was not alone in wanting to resolve the situation in these difficult negotiations. Gauguin became involved, as well as Degas's friend Henri Rouart. Raffaëlli's participation was again an issue. Degas refused to relinquish his support for Raffaëlli. As a result, Gauguin announced his intention to resign from the group in a letter he wrote to Pissarro on December 14, 1881: "Every year an Impressionist has left to be replaced by worthless artists and students of the École des Beaux-Arts. Wait another two years and you will be left alone among the lowest of the low. This will be end of all your efforts and, moreover, the end of Durand-Ruel. Despite all my good will, I can no longer act as a buffoon for Mr. Raffaëlli and Co."

Pissarro and Caillebotte started new negotiations to persuade Monet, Renoir, Cézanne, Sisley, and Berthe Morisot to take part in a group exhibition. The discussions were about to fail again when Durand-Ruel decided to use his authority with Monet, who was in favor of a restricted number of participants, and Renoir, who always feared the "revolutionary" aspect of the Independents' exhibitions. The show might never have happened, were it not for the economic conditions created by the collapse of the Union Générale bank, whose director, Jules Feder, had been one of Durand-Ruel's backers. Caillebotte accepted to participate provided that Monet did also. Pissarro wrote to Monet and submitted a list of eight names: Monet,

58. Pissarro to Caillebotte, *Correspondance de Camille Pissarro, 1865-1885*, vol. 1, ed. by Jeanine Bailly-Herzberg, Paris: Presses Universitaires de France, 1980, pp. 145-146, letter 86.

The Bezique Game, 1880
Oil on canvas
49⅞" × 63⅜" (121 × 161 cm)
Private collection
Photo Galerie Brame et
Lorenceau, Paris

59.   Pissarro to Monet, around February 24, 1882, *ibid.*, p. 155, letter 98.

60.   Armand Sallanches, «L'Exposition des artistes indépendants», *Le Journal des Arts*, March 3, 1882.

Renoir, Sisley, Pissarro, Berthe Morisot, Guillaumin, Vignon, Gauguin, and Cézanne.   He added: "Caillebotte agreed with me about this list, which presents a coherent group holding the same ideas on art with varying degrees of talent.   We cannot demand that everybody be equal in talent and it would be a great achievement if nobody marred the quality of the show."[59]

The exhibition opened on March 1, 1882, at No. 251 Rue Saint-Honoré, without Degas and without Cézanne, as the latter was showing at the Salon for the first time, thanks to the influence of his friend Guillemet, who was on the jury.   Manet had been invited by Pissarro, but he had kept to his original position despite some hesitations which were mentioned in a letter written by Manet's brother Eugène to his wife Berthe Morisot.   Caillebotte recovered his enthusiasm and energy and he played a major part in the installation of the paintings.   The quality of the exhibition was very high; it attracted a sizable crowd and drew critical acclaim.

The Bezique Game was shown at the seventh Impressionist exhibition of 1882.   The composition depicts the artist's brother Martial, smoking a meerschaum pipe, and several friends who have been identified, among them Paul Hugot sitting on a sofa in the background, whose portrait was also painted by Caillebotte.   The game is at its height, and the players have an air of quiet concentration: "One wonders who will win", a critic noted.[60] The scene evokes traditional genre-painting but it is transformed by a serious atmosphere appropriate to the social standing of the players.   One of the most interesting aspects of Caillebotte's realism is that he captures a specific social class which, while it was his class in the strict sense of the word, was also part of the rest of society by the practice of games of cards and belonged to a history which is difficult to outline.   Cézanne subsequently explored this motif as well.   They are modest and wealthy bourgeois, farmers and people of independent means, all men smoking their pipes, shuffling cards, coming into contact with one another, ignoring one another, revealing the differences between them.   Here again, Caillebotte's vision is an occasion for a sudden awareness.

Balconies of Haussmann-style buildings are representative of the values of urban life as they were defined during the Second Empire in France.   Caillebotte may have felt this more than any other painter and he developed a new dialogue between man and public areas.   More than any other, he created a relationship between the eyes and the function of architecture as a part of consistent structure.   The balcony of the building at

61. 1880, private collection, Paris.

62. 1880, private collection, Switzerland.

31 Boulevard Haussmann, curving over the Rue Scribe, allowed for open views above the trees of the boulevard.   Unlike Monet when he painted *Boulevard des Capucines*, Caillebotte structured his compositions along the straight lines of the avenues.   *The Man on the Balcony* frames the profile of a figure in the perspective view toward Saint-Augustin church.   Another, more elaborate, painting *A Balcony, Boulevard Haussmann* takes a perspective view in the opposite direction, insisting on the virtual freedom of the viewer who can detach his gaze from the figures and escape above the rooftops.[61] Shown at the exhibition of 1882, *The Man on the Balcony* brings to mind *Young Man at the Window* of 1876, in a more ambitious version in which the freedom of the brushstrokes and the light soften the bold cropping, most visibly in the strip of striped awning hanging against the sky.[62] The figure here takes over the space with great authority but this dimension is opposed to the straight lines made by the balconies.   As a result, the man acquires a new identity as he stands above the crowd but could also lose himself in it, as everything in his demeanor indicates.

We reach a sort of completeness with *View Taken From a Balcony*.   The motif of the railing becomes the unexpected theme of a landscape; it is both a screen, cutting out the landscape seen from above and leading the eyes downward, and a full-fledged ornament endowed with a symbolic value similar to that of ornaments in Renaissance paintings (see pages 96-97).   This composition should not be mistaken for a preparatory study.   This is a landscape in its own right, which presents to the viewer an exploration of two levels, both merging and overturning the traditional notion of a subject.   The painting creates a new combination of distance and nearness, symmetry and dissymmetry, darkness and light, fragmented and complete view, ornamental and functional elements.   The artist discovered a sort of realist hieroglyph, a sign expressing the strange components of the city which are poetic and rarely seen.   Van Gogh, Seurat, and Cézanne subsequently took this viewpoint as a pure expression of aesthetic sensation and subjective presence which are related to the artist moving and altering the limits and the order of forms.

The viewer's interest is similarly shifted in *A Traffic Island, Boulevard Haussmann* (see pages 98-99).   Its theme seems to call on the most banal aspect of contemporary street design.   The banality itself becomes an occasion for thoughts and a statement.   Motion and immobility are suggested by the blurred or well-defined shapes of three pedestrians, as they stand

The Man on the Balcony
Ca 1880
Oil on canvas
45⅝" × 35½" (116 × 90 cm)
Private collection
Photo Giraudon, Vanves

View Taken From a
Balcony, 1880
Oil on canvas
25⅝" × 21¼" (65 × 54 cm)
Private collection

The vision of things

at three different spots suggesting three different moments of perception. The view shifts entirely to the intersection of Boulevard Haussmann, Rue Scribe, and the Rue Gluck. The very absence of any event and the emptiness created by a refined composition seem to make it possible for something to happen. The passer-by, with whom the artist always identified somewhat, becomes the focus of a configuration which is both still and random. The harmonious colors and light brushstrokes create a sort of perpetual motion within a defined space. The lampposts mark a rhythm on the circular traffic island, evoking the face of a sundial placed in the unexpected shape of a small world leading to another world. The latter is open and expanding, its center is everywhere, and its circumference is nowhere. It is a world where anxiety is kept in check, if only in the form of a traffic island.

63. 1880, private collection, Paris.

This new approach may rely on everyday experience but it is an adventurous visual exploration. It acquires a new dimension in *Boulevard Seen From Above*,[63] in which Caillebotte creates an astonishing effect with an inverted perspective view centered on a tree and its light spring foliage. The tree appears to be growing from the air. The city is everywhere around it like the grate protecting its base. Caillebotte's Impressionism invents new relationships between the urban structure and the sovereign order of life. The viewer can see a horse, a tree, and passers-by. They exist but in a world that seems to have been suddenly changed. Paintings uncovered this mutation and, for a long time, they provided photographers, and twentieth-century photographers in particular, with both inspiration and observation.

Like Fantin-Latour, Monet, and Manet, Caillebotte knew well that a still-life was an exercise in technical mastery which must abide by the rules of a genre. The realism of the 1860s made it a decisive component of his aesthetic approach. In fact, he produced several conventional still-lifes.

He explored new possibilities, however, with a series of paintings, among them *Fruits Displayed on a Stand* (see pages 100-101). The picture describes a greengrocer's display of fruits as it is presented to passers-by. The view from above stages the display as in real life, it is not a gratuitous effect. The fruits are not placed according to an arrangement decided by the artist, but are distributed on the stand by the shopkeeper. The title of the painting suggests the usual organization of a market: fruits, vegetables, fish, poultry, etc... The painting deals with goods which are meant to be

A Traffic Island
Boulevard Haussmann
Ca 1880
Oil on canvas
31⅞" × 39¾" (81 × 101 cm)
Private collection
Photo Giraudon, Vanves

Fruits Displayed
on a Stand, 1880-1882
Oil on canvas
31⅛" × 39⅝"
(76.5 × 100.5 cm)
Museum of Fine Arts,
Boston
Mason Fund
in Memory of Alice Thevin

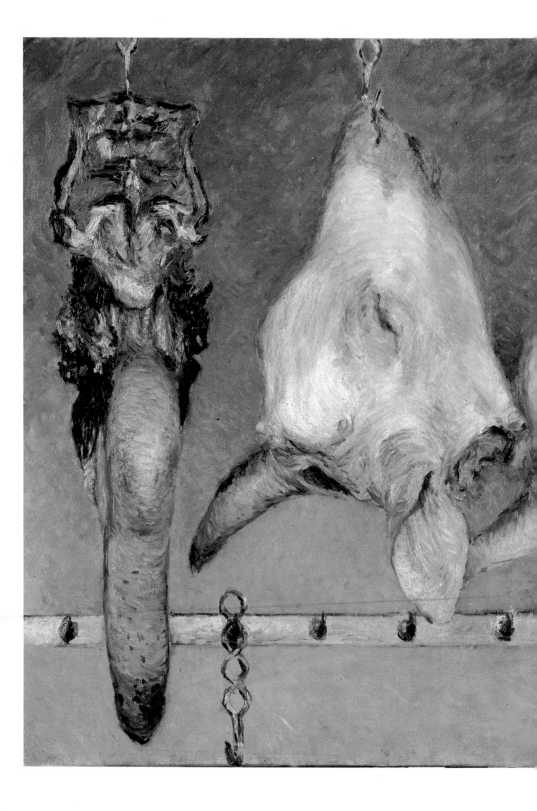

Calf's Head
and Cow's Tongue, 1882
Oil on canvas
28 11/16" × 21 1/4" (73 × 54 cm)
Private collection
Photo Galerie Brame et
Lorenceau, Paris

sold; it evokes the way people look at things in general. This is a luxury display, with high-quality fruit presented on a bed of white paper and a background of green plants. Nevertheless, the artist's approach refers to a state prior to the requirements of good taste, as they create an image which, however real it may seem, is an idealized one to the detriment of the more creative notion of merchandise.

The still-lifes with poultry and rabbits displayed in a shop confirm that Caillebotte intended to capture raw facts by framing and cropping the image in a most effective manner (see pages 136-137). A painting of a stand in a tripe-shop marks an even more decisive step in the exploration of our connection with things and material civilization; calves' heads and cows' tongues uncover something which, now as ever, is usually somewhat censored.

Clearly, Caillebotte contributed to the transformation of the concept of portrait painting by creating a distance that revealed a deep relationship with social values. He also made realist portraits as his friends Manet and Degas understood them. The portrait of the Chinese scholar Henry Cordier (1849-1925) shows his ability to establish, like Degas and Manet, a dialogue with a major tradition in French painting (see pages 104-105). The personality of this learned man is circumscribed mostly by our curiosity about an erudite China specialist whose "Biblioteca sinica" was awarded the Prix Stanislas Julien in 1880 and who was made a member of the Institut de France in 1908. The man, working in total absorption, acquires a dignity entirely due to the intellectual scope of his personality. He had traveled to the East and his writings contributed to the opening of the Eastern world toward the West. Caillebotte expressed a familiarity with a circle of high culture but he chose a new cultural field, directed toward a civilization which was still relatively unknown and subsequently held a powerful attraction for artists, musicians, and writers in the course of major political upheavals.

Portrait of a Man Writing at His Desk, dated 1885, is more surprising in its constructive form (see pages 118-1194). The man, about whom we wish we could know more, expresses the thankless concentration of a scribe absorbed in his work. The caricatural picture of a bald head with prominent ears, smoking a pipe, leads the viewer directly to the hard work of a library in Paris. This is quite different from the inspired presence of Manet's *Mallarmé*[64] or Degas's *Duranty*.[65] In its very sharpness, however, the observation suggests the complicity of a friend

64. 1876, Musée d'Orsay,
Paris.

65. 1879, Glasgow Art
Gallery and Museum.
Burrell Collection.

The vision of things

Portrait of Henri Cordier
1883
Oil on canvas
23⅜" × 31½" (65 × 80 cm)
Musée d'Orsay, Paris
Photo Réunion des
Musées nationaux, Paris

who lent himself to this composition, a man sufficiently free to eschew the vanity of his personal appearance. Caillebotte seems ready to enter effortlessly the witty and friendly world of some Nabi painters.

The isolated figure and its expressive possibilities show the extent of Caillebotte's exploration of a realism in search of innovations. *A Soldier*, dated around 1879, highlights the uniform against a light background and evokes the memory of Manet's *Bugle*.[66] More directly, it brings to mind a multitude of paintings on military themes by Isidore Pils, Adolphe Yvon, Édouard Detaille, Alphonse-Marie de Neuville, and also many realist painters. Contemporary political and social events set off the familiar aspect of this figure. The decisive demeanor and strong energy of a man wearing a heavy moustache and smoking his army tobacco indicates that Caillebotte wished to establish a social type by suggesting the texture of daily life in the military, the deep interpenetration of the uniform and the man turned soldier.

Man at His Bath, Drying Himself, dated 1884, obviously features a man having just stepped out of a bathtub and drying himself vigorously (see page 135). He is standing squarely in the full light of a bathroom in a bourgeois apartment. Motion is suggested by eloquent foreshortening, the marks left by wet feet, and a solid pose, legs set apart. The bold technique, the quality of the light, and the reference to Degas's celebrated nudes bring up the problematic question of the male nude in realist paintings. In their criticism of academic models, realist painters rejected the repertory of classical figures. As a result, the male nude became conspicuously absent from their works and they took up the theme of bathers or women at a dressing-table instead. Caillebotte's insight was opening a door which had been almost closed. Subsequently the Fauve painters and the Expressionists considered this question, which even Cézanne had left more or less untackled.

A few paintings were inspired by the aimless strolls of Père Magloire at Étretat. *Père Magloire on Saint-Clair Road at Étretat*, dated 1884, creates a bold harmony between the smock of the old sailor and a warm sky hinting at the expanse of the sea (see pages 108-109). The artist's free technique produced a solitary image of an idle man who bears with him the experience of a life and place, a disillusioned and authentic experience uniting man and landscape in the same light. This is an image which could have inspired the novelist Guy de Maupassant, but also an unpolished image that keeps its secret.

Several landscapes of the 1880s were painted during the

A Soldier, ca 1879
Oil on canvas
41¾" × 29½" (106 × 75 cm)
Josefowitz Collection

66. 1866, Musée d'Orsay, Paris.

Père Magloire
on Saint-Clair Road
at Étretat, 1884
Oil on canvas
25⅝" × 21¼" (65 × 54 cm)
Private collection
Photo Giraudon, Vanves

The Bridge at Argenteuil
and the Seine, 1885
Oil on canvas
25⅝" × 32¼" (65 × 82 cm)
Josefowitz Collection

artist's visits to small resorts by the sea on the Normandy coast, the names of which are linked to a whole period in the history of Impressionism. The delicate colors of *Regatta at Villers-sur-Mer*, the feeling of open space, the clear light green of the water over the sand, could compare favorably with Monet's paintings at Pourville (see pages 114-115). It displays a great quality of execution, with the shadows of clouds creating a dynamic effect and suggesting both actual and potential changes related to the spectacle of the sea, as it is depicted directly for the viewer's contemplation. The word "regatta" may not be totally inaccurate but the boats on the horizon are mainly fishing boats. Other compositions take as a theme the charming villas scattered along the coast, in their fashionably eclectic style, their sloping gardens, and the flowers and greenery of Normandy. They provided Caillebotte with an inspiration for varied and often surprising views, combining sails and rooftops, expressing a whole experience which the novelist Marcel Proust was about to transform into the world of Balbec.

Starting in 1882, the artist stayed for long periods at a time in his house at Petit-Gennevilliers, where he finally settled when his brother Martial married in 1887. He painted there a series of landscapes which seemed to echo the beginnings of Impressionism and engage anew this dialogue between artists working on the same motif as in the old days of Argenteuil. *The Bridge at Argenteuil and the Seine* reveals an interesting approach and a series of values particular to Caillebotte's genius: the powerful perspective view framed by the iron bridge, the intensity created by the difference in scale between the figure in the painting and the viewer's vision, the subtle tonal values, especially on the left side of the painting, these are all elements adding to the dynamic power of the constructive form. Caillebotte incorporated the lessons remembered from Impressionism and remained faithful to a poetic approach which he claimed to have mastered; he also suggested, however, endless possibilities. This feeling of technical mastery and convictions is confirmed in the landscapes painted in the plain of Gennevilliers in 1884 or 1888, which make an interesting comparison with works by Vincent van Gogh or Georges Seurat.

Thus, Caillebotte's late years were both productive and innovative, despite the fact that the collective endeavor of exhibitions was not there any more to arouse his passionate ambition. His creative potential is evident in a composition transforming a perspective view of the bank of the Seine into a series of light signals made by laundry drying in the sun (see pages 120-121). This is a variation on a old theme which had been treated by Berthe Morisot and an unexpected sequel to Degas's *Washerwomen* series. The short and divided brushstrokes are perfectly adapted to the theme of the painting, which contains a reference to a reality whose existence is never suspected but always evident. It is a social reality that modifies the inspiration of the *Floor-Scrapers* without exhausting it. The light and landscape stand for an invisible human presence deciphering a visible world, unknowingly and without symbols, the most elementary signs of which the artist seems to be simply recording.

In the same order of ideas, *View of Paris* brings to mind Caillebotte's experience with Impressionism and the very nature of his inspiration establishes a connection with tradition (see page 117). In choosing the theme of Quai des Grands-Augustin with Notre-Dame outlined in the misty heat, the artist took up a favorite motif of Romantic and Realist painters. He selected a view from above and, more importantly, he achieved a feeling of open space and monumental proportions by using brushstrokes and colors which create a golden monochrome impression.

In *Small Branch of the Seine near Argenteuil*, painted at a later date, Caillebotte explored the shiny surface of a river view. He found a balance between surface and depth, as the viewer looking from one side of the painting to the other notes the particular quality in the relationship between colors, the general effect being both airy and muddy, constructed and scattered, intense and muffled. Such colors were always featured in Caillebotte's paintings but here they work within a definition of composition which is constantly changing. It should be noted again that he deserves to be appreciated in his own right. He was innovative; he discovered things which were also discovered by Monet, and he did this with qualities and a sensibility different from those of Monet. The fact is that these qualities remained somewhat unresolved and could not be confirmed in a development similar to that which Monet pursued in his *Cathedral* and *Waterlilies* series.

The Small Branch
of the Seine
Near Argenteuil, 1890
Oil on canvas
31⅞" × 24⅜" (81 × 62 cm)
Private collection
Photo Galerie Schmit
Paris

Regatta at Villers-sur-Mer
Ca 1880
Oil on canvas
29½" × 39¾" (75 × 101 cm)
Private collection
Photo Galerie Schmit
Paris

Chapter six

A "delicate matter"

The director of the Beaux-Arts, Henry Roujon, qualified the Caillebotte bequest in those terms when he received Renoir's letter dated March 11, 1894, announcing that Caillebotte had died on February 21 and left a will bequeathing the pictures he owned to the state: "A collection of about sixty paintings by Degas, Cézanne, Manet, Monet, Renoir, Pissarro, Sisley, and Millet". The Caillebotte affair began as soon as the news was announced, provoking violent reactions soon echoed in "Le Journal des Artistes": "That the state should have accepted such filth is an indication of great moral turpitude", the painter Jean-Léon Gérome declared. The words were not new: They had been heard for years but they acquired a new sharpness with time and the possibility that paintings reviled by the official Salon might enter history. The matter was not resolved before February 1896 and the paintings which had been accepted were exhibited in the new annex of the Musée du Luxembourg early in 1897. The show attracted great crowds but it was restricted to a very small space: "In a corridor", Pissarro wrote, "with paintings stuck next to one another." Polemical declarations increased in number; the Académie des Beaux-Arts, in particular, sent a letter to the Minister of Public Education putting forward its opposition to the plan and expressing its fears regarding the turn art was taking in France. The senator Hervé de Saisy spoke out to condemn an "unhealthy" and "decadent" art. In his response Henry Roujon defended the administration's attitude in the name of a "liberal eclecticism" and invoked the public's right to form an opinion. For a long time the Caillebotte affair remained a symbol of the difficult relationship between Impressionist painters and the state. A similar issue came up at the beginning of the 1980s, when a museum of nineteenth-century art was planned at Orsay in Paris, and the question of "eclecticism" was raised in terms of history and museology.   As a result, arguments around the Caillebotte bequest were reconsidered, leading to constructive conclusions that proved the correctness of his approach.   His bequest made history and it also shed light on historical contradictions and prejudice.

Gustave Caillebotte was very wealthy, which partly accounts for his collection.   However, he clearly collected as an artist aware of the part he could play, who could see beyond his own work and understand the meaning of his act in this perspective.   The impact of such a decision will never be sufficiently noted, as well as its confrontation with an established order made of prudent, reticent, or even clearly hostile feelings.   Because of the provisions in his will, which Geffroy described as "clear, clear-cut like himself", he held a significant part in a history which still had only few landmarks.   He opened a new chapter, the consequences of which extended far beyond the borders of France.

When the artist's father died on December 25, 1874, he left a fortune worth over two million francs to be shared between his widow and four children: Alfred — his son by a previous marriage, who had become a priest — René, Gustave, and Martial.   Apart from the town house in Rue de Miromesnil, he left a considerable amount of real estate — apartment buildings and farms — as well as investments, bonds, and government annuities.   At the time Caillebotte was already committed to a career as a painter; he knew some artists but he had not taken part in the first Impressionist show held at the Boulevard des Capucines.   The sudden death of his brother René on November 2, 1876, led him to make a will with an astonishing provision, probably prompted by his recent participation in the 1876 exhibition and his decision to buy paintings with the purpose of building a collection of significant works marking the collective history of the Impressionist group.

We do not have exact records of Caillebotte's acquisitions.   The dates of the paintings indicate that they were mostly bought prior to 1880.   In April 1876, Monet recorded three sales for one thousand francs to " Mr. Caillebotte, a painter ".   Several works shown at the exhibitions of 1877, 1879, and 1880 were lent by Caillebotte.   A few works entered his collection after 1882, in particular *The Balcony* and a small study *At the Races*, which he bought at the Manet sale in 1884.   It was noted that his choices were ruled by criteria of quality.   While he supported his friends and helped them financially, the selection of paintings for his collection was never

View of Paris, Sunshine
1880
Oil on canvas
39 $^9/_{16}$" × 29 $^1/_8$"
(100.5 × 74 cm)
Josefowitz Collection

contrived or speculative. The recognition and fate of significant paintings were important to him and he contributed to the subscription organized by Monet in 1890 to acquire Manet's *Olympia* on behalf of the national collection.

The will of November 3, 1876, clearly indicates the connection between his part in a group of painters known as "intransigent or impressionist" and his wish to have their paintings enter the Musée du Luxembourg at first, and later the Louvre, as was customary at the time. The two provisions regarding the short and the long terms are complementary. In either case, the purpose was to show works to the public, which it would ultimately accept. The same logic had been behind Manet's decision in 1867 to exhibit in a separate pavilion at Pont de l'Alma. Caillebotte may have read Manet's "Reasons for a solo exhibition", in which he stated that an artist needed to show his work in order to allow time for them to be accepted, as time leads to a more balanced and less passionate viewing as well as to oblivion. These ideas were born from the artists' discussions in the 1860s and had regained their relevance.

Caillebotte authorized in writing the funding "to hold, in the best possible conditions, an exhibition of the painters known as intransigent or impressionist". He mentioned, in the following order: Degas, Monet, Pissarro, Renoir, Cézanne, Sisley, Berthe Morisot. He added: "I name these without excluding others", as further proof of his generosity and a possible indication that he was still hoping that Manet would eventually take part in their exhibitions. This provision was motivated by the impending World Fair of 1878, which was already on everybody's mind and created circumstances unfavorable to the Impressionists.

The codicil dated November 23, 1883, noted that the provision regarding the 1878 exhibition had become unnecessary, without making a similar one for the future. In the meantime, the history of the Impressionist exhibitions had taught him a lesson and he only reaffirmed the second part of his original will, regarding the bequest of his collection: "I bequeath to the state the pictures I own; as I want this gift to be accepted, and accepted in such a way that the paintings go neither into an attic nor to a provincial museum but right to the Musée du Luxembourg and later to the Louvre, a certain lapse of time will be necessary before the execution of this clause, until the public may, I don't say understand, but at best admit this art. This time could be twenty years or more. In the meanwhile my brother Martial, or failing him another of my heirs, will keep the

Portrait of a Man
Writing at His Desk
(Émile-Jean Fontaine)
1885
Oil on canvas
25¹³⁄₁₆" × 32" (65.5 × 81.5 cm)
Josefowitz Collection

Laundry Drying
on the Bank of the Seine
Petit-Gennevilliers, 1888
Oil on canvas
41¾" × 59" (106 × 150 cm)
Wallraf-Richartz Museum
Cologne
Photo Rheinisches
Bildarchiv
Cologne

collection. I ask Renoir to be my executor and to accept a painting of his choice; my heirs will insist that he take an important one."

Renoir's role as an executor was confirmed in the codicil dated November 5, 1889. He was a close friend of Caillebotte, who helped him a lot. The codicil of 1883 freed Renoir of his debt. When Renoir sold *Young Girls at the Piano* to the Musée du Luxembourg in 1892, he dedicated a second version of the painting to Caillebotte. The latter was the godfather of Renoir's eldest son, Pierre, born in 1885. These ties lasted after Caillebotte's death and in 1895 Renoir painted the portrait of Martial Caillebotte's children.

We shall not consider the details of the difficult negotiations around the bequest, as the whole case involves fine points of law and also a background which highlights the difficulties raised by the gift. The bequest was both an embarrassment and an opportune development for an administration increasingly aware of the glaring gaps in its collection of contemporary art. Failure to have such works in the national collection was against the authorities' official mandate based on a "liberal eclecticism" which was threatened by the orientation of the works on view. Between the "small" paintings by Meissonier and the "great" picture by Cormon, space needed to be found for Monet, Cézanne, Degas, and Pissarro. The difficulty lay in the donor's condition that neither "an attic" nor "a province" be an acceptable solution for paintings meant to be hung in a museum which did not have enough space for the whole collection to be on view.

Caillebotte knew the Musée du Luxembourg. He had specifically indicated that his brother or another heir should keep the collection in the meantime. The museum refused to exhibit the complete collection of sixty-seven paintings and pastel drawings (plus a watercolor and a drawing by Millet) on the grounds that it lacked space and that, for reasons of fairness, each artist could only be represented by three or four works. This rejection led to long negotiations which gave rise to polemics and various interpretations. The administrative authorities wished to accept the bequest, even if it entailed making a subsequent selection. The question of a possible interpretation of Caillebotte's will was raised at the March 1894 meeting of the advisory committee to the national museums. The director of the Musée du Luxembourg, Léonce Bénédite, thought it might be possible to build a temporary construction on the museum's terrace in order to house the bequest. A solution was about to be found whereby guarantees would be given to both parties: The state could be able to choose the works which could be exhibited and Martial Caillebotte would keep the rest until adequate space would be found for the whole collection. Léonce Bénédite rejected this compromise because there was a legal problem in having a private person keeping paintings which were by law the property of the state. He proposed to abide by the provisions of the will and send the paintings which could not be on view at the Musée du Luxembourg to the castles of Compiègne and Fontainebleau, which also formed part of the national museums' trust. This would have been a distortion of the spirit of the will and Martial Caillebotte refused to hand over the collection. As it was impossible to comply with the will to the letter, a compromise was struck in January 1895 whereby the state accepted a portion of the collection and pledged to put it on view, while the other paintings became Martial Caillebotte's property. After lengthy negotiations, thirty-eight works were selected and twenty-nine were rejected. This compromise was close to the initial solution which Léonce Bénédite had refused, but this time the partition was final.

Degas's seven pastel drawings were all accepted. With Manet's *Balcony* and *Angelina*, the Musée du Luxembourg was to receive paintings whose radical realism was worthy of *Olympia*. Cézanne entered the national collection with *L'Estaque* and *Farmyard at Auvers*; unfortunately, *Bathers Resting* was rejected. Renoir was represented by masterpieces: *A Ball at the Moulin de la Galette*, *The Swing*, *Woman in the Sun*. Pissarro and Sisley were consulted on the choices to be made. Pissarro expressed some regrets for the rejection of a large landscape at Louveciennes, but on the whole he was fairly satisfied. Only eight paintings by Monet were selected out of sixteen in the collection: *Rocks at Belle-Ile* (1886) was the most recent one. *Gare Saint-Lazare* of 1877 was selected but two studies on the same motif were not. His most sunlit Impressionism was featured with *Regatta at Argenteuil* of 1872; his more austere depictions of cold weather were represented with *Church at Vétheuil* and *Frost*, both dated 1879. The Luxembourg also chose *A Corner in an Apartment* (1875), *The Luncheon* (1873), and *The Tuileries Garden* (1876), which were significant paintings for Caillebotte's inspiration. The bequest was transferred to the Louvre in 1929. In the meantime, a retrospective exhibition of Caillebotte's works was held at the Salon d'Automne in 1921. After World War II, in 1947, the Museum of Impressionism opened its doors at the Jeu de Paume.

Villas by the Sea
in Normandy, ca 1880
Oil on canvas
22⅞" × 25⅝" (58 × 65 cm)
Private collection

Chapter seven

One hundred years later

A retrospective exhibition of Caillebotte's paintings was held at the Galerie Durand-Ruel, in the Rue Le Peletier, from June 4 to June 16, 1894. Very few pictures were sold among the one hundred and twenty-three on view. Degas, who was always affected by the death of an artist, bought *Yellow Roses in a Vase*, dated 1882. He remembered that, with his friend Henri Rouart, he had set Caillebotte on his path as an independent artist. On April 27 of the same year, the state accepted the gift of *Floor-Scrapers* proposed by Renoir and Martial Caillebotte. The painting was taken to the Musée du Luxembourg in June 1896. It pointed to the fact that the artist had not included any of his own works in his bequest. Caillebotte was always described as, in Geffroy's words, " a truly rare companion, totally selfless, thinking of others before himself — if he thought of himself at all ".[67] When he died, Pissarro wrote to his son Lucien: " We have just lost another sincere, devoted friend; Caillebotte died suddenly of cerebral paralysis. He was someone we can really mourn. He was good and generous, and a talented painter to boot. "[68] Beneath Caillebotte's natural modesty, there was a sincere desire to be recognized one day in the same league as his friends, at least next to the painters he admired. Renoir's son Jean remembered that he " hoped to be deemed worthy of having his paintings hung in the space leading to the room where paintings by Renoir and Cézanne were shown ". This was a characteristically humble and clear-minded remark, which should be noted but not distorted.

Shortly before he died, his friends decided to arrange an exhibition as a homage. It took place after his death but the uproar caused by his bequest distracted the public's attention from paintings which seemed already distant in time. It had been more than ten years since Caillebotte had had a major exhibition. Despite the recognition for his work and its quality, his stature was viewed in more ambiguous terms. A

67. Gustave Geffroy, *op. cit.*, vol. II, p. 32. Quoted in Kirk Varnedoe, *op. cit.*

68. *Lettres de Pissarro à son fils Lucien*, Paris, 1943, letter dated March 1, 1894, p. 336. Quoted in Kirk Varnedoe, *ibid.*

The Piano Lesson, 1881
Oil on canvas
31⅞" × 25⅝" (81 × 65 cm)
Musée Marmottan, Paris

69. Arsène Alexandre, «Le Legs Caillebotte», *Le Paris*, March 13, 1894.

development was missing which would have placed him in the forefront of the contemporary scene. Arsène Alexandre exclaimed in 1894: "What a great painter Caillebotte would have been, what a significant place he would have held in our movement, had he not been somewhat distracted and discouraged as an artist "[69]

It is correct to say that the artist did not work with the same urgency and rhythm after 1882. He had already produced his most important paintings, even if later works of great quality showed that he was still trying to innovate. His life focused progressively on the Seine and his house at Petit-Gennevilliers. There he could indulge his two passions: gardening and boating. In the garden and its greenhouse he could devote himself to the art of horticulture, and he compared notes with Monet on the subject. Like him, he painted pictures of the flowers in his garden. He also designed boats which were famous for their refinement (sails made of silk embossed with a heraldic cat) and their amusing names (The Roastbeef, Condor, Inès, The Stringbean, Grasshopper). Several paintings evoke the regatta at Argenteuil and he depicted himself for the last time in 1893 as a helmsman, as if he were taking his leave. He was elected to the municipal council in 1888 and was happy to contribute to the well-being of the community by paying from his own purse for such public services as streetlights, road repairs, and the firemen's uniform. He never married but after about 1883 he lived with a young woman, Charlotte Berthier, who was then twenty years old — he was thirty-five. He left her a life annuity of twelve thousand francs and confirmed this provision in the 1889 codicil to his will, in which he also gave her a house. This young woman appears in the world of his garden, standing near a bed of roses in a painting of 1893 in particular. It has often been noted that Caillebotte lived a life without excessive luxury, that he valued freedom and independence, and that he needed to be active. This wealthy bourgeois was not only an artist; he could become a messenger and journeyman for his friends. After the large apartment in the Boulevard Haussmann where the two brothers had lived both "side by side and separately", Petit-Gennevilliers may have provided a setting more open to nature, work, and life. It was an ideal setting which painters could dimly perceive.

We know very little about Caillebotte's ideas. His way of life was that of a well-to-do bourgeois, with a cook, a maid (who had two children), and two sailors. We know that he was always eager to meet his friends, to overcome unnecessary differences,

Sunflowers, the Garden at Petit-Gennevilliers, 1885
Oil on canvas
52⅛" × 41⅜" (131 × 105 cm)
Private collection
Photo Giraudon, Vanves

Sailboat on the Seine
at Argenteuil, 1892
Oil on canvas
25⅝" × 21¼" (65 × 54 cm)
Private collection

Place Saint-Georges
1880-1882
Oil on canvas
28 $^{11}/_{16}$" × 36 $^{1}/_{4}$" (73 × 92 cm)
Private collection
Photo Galerie Schmit
Paris

G. Caillebotte.

and to resume interesting discussions. He displayed these qualities in a letter to Pissarro, when the latter declined an invitation to a banquet in honor of Manet in 1885, one year after the retrospective exhibition which had been held at the École des Beaux-Arts after Manet had died. Caillebotte wrote: "We all agree that this banquet is meaningless", but he reminded Pissarro that it was important because of Manet: "We do not wish to be accused of ingratitude or ill-will toward Manet, especially since we may be his only true admirers among everybody present. In short, we are all going. I know you wrote that you would not attend, but it doesn't matter. I will take care of that." He felt a strong need to say "we", to belong to a community, to work together, and this aspect of his personality may raise some questions. Solitude did not foster his creativity. He longed for a creative intensity in a collective framework. He was deeply wounded by conflicts and individual susceptibilities. He wrote before the exhibition in 1882: "I feel disgusted, I am retiring to my tent".[70]

Caillebotte's work took a long time to be discovered again. Although France owed him a large debt, he was forgotten for a long while and relegated to the role of a minor figure. A few turning points occurred in the 1960s, when in 1966 Michel Monet bequested the paintings which his father had owned, including a sketch for *Paris Street, Rainy Day*, and when the Wildenstein Galleries put on a show in London in 1966 and in New York in 1968. In 1964, the Art Institute in Chicago purchased Caillebotte's most ambitious painting, *Paris Street, Rainy Day*. Mention should also be made of the definitive work by Marie Berhaut, published in 1978, and the role of such American art historians as Robert Rosenblum, Peter Galassi, or Kirk Varnedoe, who put forward a new approach to Caillebotte's paintings. This renewed interest was followed by more complete and precise studies of the history of Impressionism and its aesthetic and social content. Between the retrospective exhibition held in Houston and Brooklyn in 1976 and the centenary show organized in Paris and Chicago in 1994, the history of the nineteenth century has been reassessed and Caillebotte's work has acquired a new meaning.

To define his role does not mean that he should always been compared to others. He should not be treated as if he did not exist in his own right and was only there to set off other painters. He was a creative and sincere artist. He sought to innovate and painted a few masterpieces which make

70. Undated letter from Caillebotte to Pissarro, in Marie Berhaut, *op. cit.*, pp. 246-247, quoted in Kirk Varnedoe, *op. cit.*

Impressionism as we see it. He should not be dwarfed by the towering example of Manet, Degas, Renoir, or Monet. He was not a minor master either. We can perceive his ambition, with its risks and accomplishments. Removing him from a circle which he claimed to be his and comparing him to such realist painters as James Tissot, Giuseppe De Nittis, Thomas Eakins, or Max Klinger seem unnecessary. An interpretation of his paintings based on the works of Caspar David Friedrich and the hyper-realists appears equally doubtful and contrived. To highlight the components of his realist style which are close to that of the Salon painters would amount to a betrayal of his purpose. Gustave Caillebotte had his own place in the history in which he played a part. He was his own man next to his friends, Renoir, Pissarro, Monet, who recognized his talent and loved him. The question remains whether he had his place in "the space leading to the main exhibition room" or in the room itself. It may be in both places, but he certainly did not deserve to be forgotten and neglected or perpetually compared with someone else.

He created a unique world to which he alone could give a life, a colored light which is immediately recognizable, and an observation which contains the direct understanding of a complete story. His universe is both familiar and strange. It is marked by a lack of something, an absence which proved to be creative. It is a world of unmarried men, organized around a solitude and remoteness that are part of freedom. Caillebotte painted elegant young women, wives, relatives, and even a nude. But the female theme is part of a larger idea or scheme and it did not possess this quality of aesthetic energy which all his friends sought to depict. Caillebotte did not follow the Impressionist movement in its most attractive pleasures. He even denied himself strong emotions in the face of nature. He approached the sublime quality of light very carefully. He may have discovered the power of light but he kept it concealed, veiled. The essence of his work was related to the bourgeois world around him: his family, its houses and habits, the society to which it belonged, the modern city and its extensions in the country or by the sea. His paintings reflected in part the realist program which had been described and articulated on several occasions. Their modernity must be viewed objectively in the light of the logical approach that had made it possible. Caillebotte's talent, his honesty and clear-mindedness indicated also a sort of critical awareness. There was a desire for truth which may have neglected a deeper truth. One could

Reclining Nude, ca 1880
Oil on canvas
51" × 77" (128.5 × 195.6 cm)
The Minneapolis
Institute of Arts
John R. Van Derlip Fund

outline the barrier which always stood between his power of analysis and his emotions, a somewhat violent boldness and a need for rational control, a technical virtuosity and an art that is simplified, even standardized.

His most significant contribution was an innovative depiction of the relationship between the bourgeoisie and the working classes. The floor-scrapers, the house painters, the workers in their smock represent a world which is close, stripped of any rhetorical idealization, holding a function which makes it both a part of modern society and more clearly defined as a social class. Caillebotte's logical approach led him to depict the heterogeneous character of society. Before his relatives, his friends, his equals, extreme proximity triggered a feeling of difference, or even indifference. The figures in his paintings look away and their existence is never challenged by the viewer's gaze, as it is simply relying on the walls around them. The transparency of the visible world is pushed to its limits and reinforces this effective social barrier. Sometimes the truth stirs to life; it seems to rebel and becomes bolder and sharper, but it stands against a definitive order, an organization of the world which can be observed but is set for a long time. The visible reality cannot be separated from its shape. The window, the balcony, the street, the determined viewpoints always imply the artist's objective presence. Caillebotte created an illusion of truth. His method aimed at a representational imitation which shaped his technique. He conceived of a scene or a perspective view and he adapted it to his figures; the latter were first carefully studied in their posture, their movements, and their specific details.

One may wonder whether he used photography as a model. His brother Martial was an amateur photographer. Despite certain effects in his paintings, however, there is no document to prove that he used photographs. The foreshortening of some perspective constructions could be obtained with a simple optical box and the analysis of his paintings shows that their composition could not be reduced to that of a photograph. It could be said that Caillebotte painted to obtain a more expressive photograph of a subject, to create colors and achieve a colored sensation. Duranty alluded to this in 1876 when he noted that realist painters do not wish to record "a meaningless pose before a photographer's lens". He believed that photography could incite painters to sharpen their observation and create adequate new techniques. "Suppose, for instance, that at a given moment

Man at His Bath
Drying Himself, 1884
Oil on canvas
67⅜" × 49¼"
(170.1 × 125 cm)
Josefowitz Collection

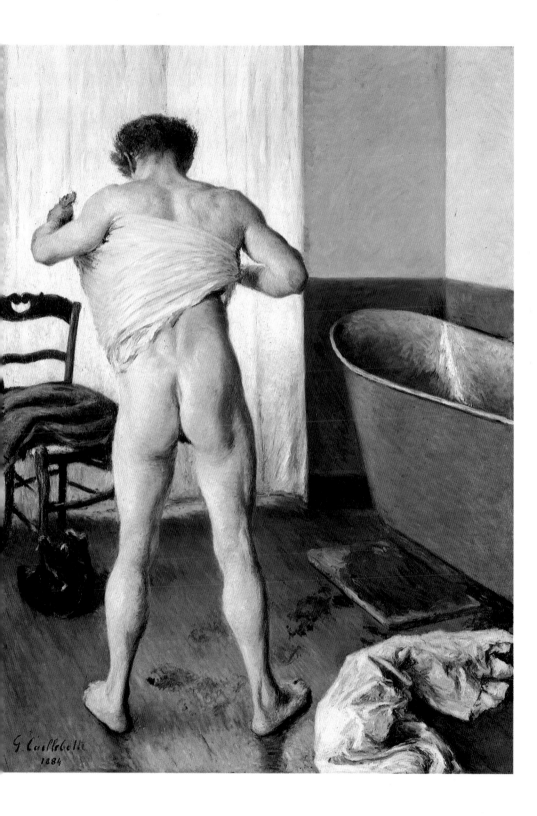

G. Caillebotte
1884

Still Life
Display of Chickens
and Game Birds, 1882
Oil on canvas
29⅞" × 41⅜" (76 × 105 cm)
Private collection

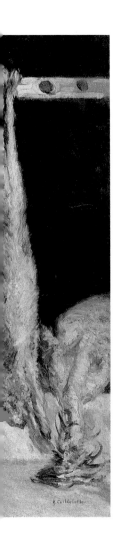

we could take a color photograph of an interior. We would have a perfect match, a true and real representation, with every element expressing the same feeling. Suppose then that we waited and, when the sun was covered by a cloud, we immediately took another picture. The result would be similar to the first. It is up to observation to compensate for these instantaneous means of execution that we do not possess and to preserve the memory of the images they would have rendered."

Both Duranty and Huysmans noted that Caillebotte captured a reality cut out of a precise moment in time, a moment in life which expressed the unexpected and infinitely varied aspect of the real world. He was a skillful user of the celebrated technique of cropping images, exploring and discovering the visible world by abolishing conventions which had become ineffective. He was a colorist who invented a range of gray and blue tones that imparted a unique character to the whole painting, as well as harmonies of strong and austere colors which were attuned to the very nature of his vision. His "ingenuity" was contained in that which he showed to the viewer, that is a reality both human and inhuman which he found in the heart of Realism. He may have been disillusioned as an Impressionist but he did not venture into a more active and direct approach. His art may seem confident and based on reason, but it also masked a element of melancholy. From this point of view, Caillebotte was a contemporary of the naturalists. His significance lies in his unique contribution to a group also known as independent. His paintings seem to provide the material for the long-range history of a world in mutation, for which Paris was a model in the nineteenth century. Some of his paintings bring to mind the writings of Walter Benjamin. In fact, the history of photographers, critics, and painters of the twentieth century make us perceive Caillebotte as a pioneer. And this is never something of minor importance.

Eric Darragon

Portrait of Jules Froyez
Ca 1879
Oil on canvas
31 7⁄8" × 25 5⁄8" (81 × 65 cm)
Private collection
Photo Galerie Brame et
Lorenceau, Paris

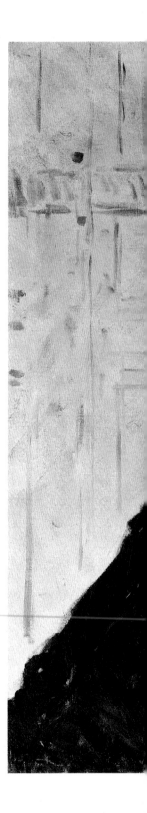

Chronology

1848 Gustave Caillebotte was born in Paris, in the Rue du Faubourg Saint-Denis, on August 19. His mother, Céleste Daufresne (born in 1819), was the daughter of a lawyer from Lisieux. His father, Martial Caillebotte (born in 1799), was a native of Normandy. The family's wealth came from a successful business supplying cloth and blankets to the French army. The family store, "Le Lit militaire", was at No. 160 Rue du Faubourg Saint-Denis, in an older part of Paris.

1850 His brother René was born.
The family moved to No. 152 Rue du Faubourg Saint-Denis, in a large one-family house with a garden.

1853 His brother Martial was born.

February 1848 The House of Orléans was overthrown by revolution and the Second Republic was proclaimed.
The government responded to the artists' wish that an elected jury select the paintings for the Salon. For the first time, the Barbizon artists took part in the Salon.

1850 The Salon confirmed the triumph of landscape painting.

1852 Beginning of the Second Empire. The new regime's military expenditure contributed to the great wealth of Caillebotte's family.
A painting by Théodore Rousseau entered the collection of the Musée du Luxembourg.

1853-1855 Degas entered the studio of Barrias. Later he studied under Lamothe, a follower of Ingres.

1855 Manet entered the studio of Couture at the École des Beaux-Arts.
Pissarro left the West Indies and arrived in Paris. He worked at the École des Beaux-Arts and the Académie Suisse. Met Corot. The World Fair presented a wide selection of works by Ingres, Delacroix and Rousseau. The jury accepted 11 paintings by Courbet but it rejected *The Burial* and *The Studio*. Courbet decided to build a

Pavilion of Realism at his own expense, where he showed 40 paintings.
A painting by Corot entered the collection of the Musée du Luxembourg.

1856 Manet left Couture's studio and traveled abroad.
Edgar Degas traveled to Italy.
Pissarro worked in the countryside around Paris.
Cézanne studied painting in Gibert's studio at the museum of Aix-en-Provence.

1857 Entered the Lycée Louis-le-Grand, where he was an excellent liberal arts student.

1857 The art critic Castagnary gave a definition of Naturalism as opposed to Realism.

1859 Manet was rejected from the Salon despite Delacroix's intervention in his favor.
Courbet organized a celebration of Realism on October 1.

1860 His father purchased a beautiful country house at Yerres, in the Seine-et-Oise district, close to Paris and in a particularly pleasant area.

1860 Monet enrolled in the Académie Suisse.
Manet's paintings at the Salon were well received by the critics.
Pissarro was rejected from the Salon.
Berthe Morisot studied under Corot.

1861 Courbet created an academy of Realism in Paris, but he soon lost interest in teaching.
Pissarro met Cézanne and Guillaumin at the Académie Suisse.

1862 Beginning of a long friendship between Degas and Manet. The latter introduced Degas to Renoir, Monet, and Zola.
Monet, Renoir, Sisley, and Bazille met in Gleyre's studio.
Gatherings at the Café de Bade and later at the Café Guerbois.

1863 Exhibition of the Salon des Refusés, with works by Manet, Pissarro, Jongkind, Guillaumin, Whistler, and Cézanne (whose name was not listed in the catalogue).
Pissarro's landscapes were favorably reviewed by Castagnary.
Cézanne named Courbet, Manet, and Delacroix as his masters.
Monet, Renoir, Sisley, and Bazille left Gleyre's studio to paint together in the forest of Fontainebleau, where they met Diaz de la Peña.
Delacroix died.
Baudelaire published "Le Peintre de la vie moderne" in "Le Figaro".

1864-1870 Cézanne's submissions to the Salon were consistently rejected.

1865 Monet met Courbet at Trouville.
Renoir painted with Sisley at Marlotte.

1866 Despite the support of Corot and Daubigny, *Mère Anthony's Tavern* by Renoir was rejected by the Salon.
Renoir painted with Monet in Paris and worked in Bazille's studio.
Cézanne met Manet, who liked his still-lifes.

1867 On the occasion of the World Fair in Paris, Courbet and Manet built their own respective pavilion to show their work. Manet's exhibition was not very successful.
Pissarro, Renoir, Sisley, and Bazille signed a petition requesting another Salon des Refusés.
Rousseau died.

1868 His family moved to a town house in a newly built residential section of the city, at 77 Rue de Miromesnil, in the eighth *arrondissement.* Subsequently Caillebotte arranged a studio there.

1869 Caillebotte received his bachelor's degree in law. After a brief period of military service, during which he was stationed in Strasbourg and Rouen, his family purchased a replacement to serve for him from June 1869 to June 1870, while he continued his studies.

1870 He received his law degree on July 23. He was called up for active duty for nine months in the Garde mobile of the Seine district. After the war, he decided against a career in law and enrolled in the studio of the painter Léon Bonnat, who may have introduced him subsequently to Degas.

1868 Manet, Degas, Pissarro, Monet, Renoir, Sisley, Bazille, and Morisot were accepted at the Salon. Odilon Redon and Zola wrote favorable reviews.

1869 Renoir painted with Monet at Bougival.

1870 Degas, Pissarro, Renoir, Sisley, Bazille, and Berthe Morisot were accepted at the Salon. Cézanne did not submit any painting. The jury's rejection of Monet's submission prompted Daubigny to resign.
War was declared against Prussia in July. The German army routed the French. The Third Republic was proclaimed in September.
Bazille was killed in combat.

1871 Paris was occupied by German forces on January 29. The armistice treaty triggered a popular insurrection. The revolutionary Commune seized power in March but was defeated shortly thereafter, on May 28.
In the wake of this political upheaval the standards of the jury became increasingly conservative.
Pissarro and Monet met the dealer Paul Durand-Ruel, whose gallery featured the Barbizon artists. The following year Durand-Ruel met Manet, Sisley, and Degas, whose works he subsequently exhibited in his gallery.

1872 Caillebotte made the requisite trip to Italy. Became a friend of Giuseppe De Nittis.
Painted his first known works, among them *A Road Near Naples.*

1873 Passed the entrance examination to the École des Beaux-Arts in March as a student of Bonnat.
First dated work, *Reclining Nude.*

1872 Durand-Ruel bought 32 paintings from Manet.
Pissarro and Cézanne worked together after nature.

1873 Beginning of an economic recession which made the situation of non-conformist artists increasingly difficult.
Another Salon des Refusés featured 477 participants.
Pissarro, Monet, and Sisley did not submit works to the Salon.
Creation of the cooperative named "Société anonyme à capital variable des artistes peintres, sculpteurs, graveurs, etc.", whose purpose was to organize exhibitions without a screening before a jury nor the aim of winning an award, sell the works from the show, and publish a journal devoted exclusively to the arts. It was liquidated after the first exhibition.
Some collectors began to show interest in the works of Manet and the Impressionists: Théodore Duret, the industrialist and painter Henri Rouart, Valpinçon, Caillebotte, Ernest Hoschedé, Dr. Gachet.

1874 It can be assumed that Caillebotte saw the first Impressionist exhibition and that he met its artists through Degas.
His father died on December 25, leaving a considerable fortune to his sons.

1874 Hoschedé must sell some of his paintings at auction at the Hôtel Drouot.
First Impressionist exhibition in Nadar's studio, at 35 Boulevard des Capucines, with 160 paintings by 30 artists, among them Boudin (6 works), Cals, Degas (10 works) Cézanne (3 works), Guillaumin (3 works), Monet (9 works), Morisot (9 works), De Nittis (5 works), Pissarro (5 works), Renoir (7 works) and Sisley (5 works). Degas had insisted that some more conventional

artists, who were accepted by the Salon, be also invited to join. Corot, Courbet, and Manet did not take part in the exhibition. Cézanne's paintings provoked the public's harshest comments. The show attracted a few new collectors: Dr. de Bellio, the publisher Georges Charpentier, Count Armand Doria, and Victor Chocquet, a government employee of modest means who had already assembled a collection of works by Delacroix.

Durand-Ruel exhibited works by the Impressionists in London.

1875 Stayed in Naples with De Nittis.

His *Floor-Scrapers* were rejected by the Salon.

Auction sale of Impressionists paintings at the Hôtel Drouot. Caillebotte bought *Corner of an Apartment* by Monet.

1876 Renoir and Rouart invited Caillebotte to take part in the second Impressionist exhibition. Caillebotte showed 8 works, among them the two versions of *Floor-Scrapers*, *Young Man at the Piano*, *Young Man at the Window*, and *Luncheon*. Several critics viewed him as a student of Degas.

His brother René died on November 2.

Caillebotte made a will bequeathing the pictures he owned to the state, indicating that they should remain with his brother Martial for a period of twenty years and subsequently exhibited at the Musée du Luxembourg, at the expense of his heirs. His collection featured works by Degas (pastel drawings), Cézanne, Manet, Monet, Renoir, Pissarro, Sisley, and Millet. He asked Renoir to be his executor.

1875 Millet and Corot died.

Cézanne was rejected by the Salon but he did not feel sufficiently close to the Impressionists to take part in their second exhibition.

1876 Second Impressionist exhibition at No. 11 Rue Le Peletier, in the rooms of the Galerie Durand-Ruel. It featured 19 artists, among them Cals (10 works), Degas (24 works), Monet (18 works), Morisot (17 works), Pissarro (12 works), Renoir (18 works), and Sisley (8 works). In an essay on the new painting, which was also a review of the exhibition, the critic Edmond Duranty praised the Naturalism illustrated by Caillebotte and Degas.

Gauguin started a collection of works by Manet, Cézanne, Renoir, Monet, Sisley, Guillaumin, Jongkind, and Daumier.

Paid the rent for the studio where Monet painted his series on *Gare Saint-Lazare.*

1877 Caillebotte took the initiative of the third Impressionist exhibition, which he organized with great rigor, without concessions to dealers, critics, or collectors, and he was careful to include every artist associated with the Impressionist movement. He failed to convince Manet to join the group. He showed 6 paintings, among them *Paris Street, Rainy Day, Pont de l'Europe, The House Painters, Portrait of Madame Martial Caillebotte,* and *Portraits in the Country.* Among the paintings shown at the exhibition, three paintings by Pissarro, one by Renoir, one by Monet, and three pastel drawings by Degas came from his collection. He bought Renoir's *Ball at the Moulin de la Galette* and three versions of the *Gare Saint-Lazare* by Monet.

His own work in pastels was inspired by Degas' pastel drawings.

Caillebotte was a significant buyer at the sales of Impressionist paintings. He bought back his own works and it appears that he paid more than the set price for paintings by his Impressionist friends, thus indirectly increasing the group's profits from the sale.

1878 Caillebotte failed in his efforts to organize a fourth Impressionist exhibition.

Paintings of rowing and bathing scenes, the theme and technique of which were more clearly Impressionist and evoked the paintings by Monet, Renoir, and Manet at Argenteuil.

His mother died.

1877 Third Impressionist exhibition at No. 6 Rue Le Peletier, with 241 works by 18 artists, among them Cals (10 works), Cézanne (who did not take part in another Impressionist exhibition and whose 16 works caused an uproar), Degas (26 works), Guillaumin (8 works), Monet (30 works), Morisot (12 works), Pissarro (22 works), Renoir (21 works), and Sisley (17 works). The exhibition was well received but sales were poor.

Second auction sale of Impressionist paintings at the Hôtel Drouot (Renoir, Pissarro, Sisley, and Caillebotte).

Hoschedé was declared bankrupt.

Degas invited Mary Cassatt to join the Impressionist group.

Courbet died.

Gatherings at the Café de La Nouvelle Athènes.

1878 The Impressionists decided not to hold an exhibition because of the public's greater interest in the World Fair.

Théodore Duret published his book on the Impressionist painters.

Auction sale of the Hoschedé collection in June.

Daubigny died.

1879 Sent 25 works to the fourth Impressionist exhibition, among them 6 pastel drawings and the oarsmen series.

The family house on the bank of the river Yerres and the town house in the Rue de Miromesnil were sold. Caillebotte and his brother Martial moved to an apartment in the Boulevard Haussmann, behind the Opera House. He painted a series of plunging views of the city, and scenes seen from a window or a balcony.

Caillebotte contributed to the organization of the fourth Impressionist exhibition. Mainly, he collected the works of Monet and had them framed for the show.

1879 Major exhibition of the Barbizon painters at Durand-Ruel's.

Fourth Impressionist exhibition at No. 28 Avenue de l'Opéra, which claimed to be a show of independent artists rather than Impressionists. Degas established as a condition for participation that the artists forsake the Salon. Cézanne, Renoir, and Sisley felt that, for financial reasons, they could not abide by this condition. The exhibition featured around 264 works (18 not listed in the catalogue) by 15 artists, among them Cals (14 works), Mary Cassatt (11 works), Degas (25 works listed in the catalogue), Monet (29 works), and Pissarro (38 works). Gauguin was invited to take part in the show by Degas and Pissarro and he presented a few sculptures.

Disagreements regarding the break with the Salon and the acceptance of new participants drove the Impressionists apart.

Daumier died.

1880 Bought a house at Petit-Gennevilliers, near Argenteuil. Until 1887, Caillebotte spent the spring and summer months at Petit-Gennevilliers, and the autumn and winter months in Paris.

Caillebotte disagreed strongly with Degas about the organization of the next Impressionist exhibition and the selection of new participants. He showed 11 paintings, among them *In an Café, Interior, Woman at the Window*, which was highly praised by the writer J.-K. Huysmans and by Signac, *View of Paris, Sunshine, Interior, Woman Reading*, and 3 pastel drawings.

He lost heart in the face of internal dissension in the Impressionist group and his production waned.

1880 Fifth Impressionist exhibition at No. 10 Rue des Pyramides. Renoir, Sisley, Cézanne, and Monet did not take part. Fifteen artists were featured, among them Cassatt (8 paintings and a series of prints), Degas (11 paintings, drawings, and a series of etchings listed in the catalogue), Gauguin (8 works, among them 7 paintings made at Pontoise with Pissarro), Guillaumin (22 works), Morisot (8 works), and Pissarro (11 paintings and a series of prints). The group, however, had lost its cohesion and too many participants were artists of lesser talent.

Manet may have seen *In a Café*, which shows similarities with his own *Bar at the Folies-Bergère* of 1882.

1881 He did not take part in the sixth Impressionist exhibition.
After this date, he painted fairly often on the coast of Normandy.

1881 The disagreement between Caillebotte and Degas reached new heights. Caillebotte failed to convince Degas to distance himself from the less-talented artists whom he had invited to join the group and to put on an exhibition based on more stringent artistic criteria. He played a significant part in the organization and installation of the exhibition, but he had to take into account the commercial needs of Durand-Ruel. He showed 18 works, among them *The Bezique Game*, *Fruits Displayed on a Stand*, and *Boulevard Seen from Above*. Critics praised his paintings with figures more than his more experimental plunging views. Caillebotte did not exhibit in Paris again during his lifetime.

1883 Bought Manet's *Balcony*. It was one of his last important acquisitions.
Wrote a first codicil to his will, dated November 23, in which he reaffirmed the

1881 Sixth Impressionist exhibition at No. 35 Boulevard des Capucines, in which Caillebotte, Cézanne, Monet, Renoir, and Sisley did not take part. This exhibition may be regarded as the triumph of Degas' concept of realism in Impressionism. It featured 13 artists, among them Cassatt (11 works), Degas (8 works, including the sculpture of the little dancer), Gauguin (10 works), Guillaumin (16 works), Morisot (7 works), and Pissarro (28 works).
Durand-Ruel resumed buying works from the Impressionists.

1881 Seventh Impressionist exhibition at No. 251 rue Saint-Honoré. It was entitled an "Exhibition of independent artists". Degas and Cassatt did not take part. It featured eight artists, among them Gauguin (13 works), Guillaumin (26 works, including 13 pastel drawings), Monet (35 works), Morisot (12 works, including 3 not listed in the catalogue), Pissarro (34 works), Renoir (27 works, including 2 not listed in the catalogue), and Sisley (27 works). It was the last exhibition reflecting the composition and preoccupations of the original Impressionist group as it gave pride of place to landscapes and plein-air paintings.

1882 Georges Petit founded a yearly international exhibition.
A painting by Cézanne was accepted at the Salon thanks to the support of Guillemet. It attracted little notice.

1883 Manet died.
Durand-Ruel organized a series of one-man exhibitions of Impressionist painters in London, Boston, Berlin, and Rotterdam. His

bequest of his collection to the state on condition that these works go neither into an attic nor to a provincial museum but right to the Musée du Luxembourg and later to the Louvre. He made complete remittance to Renoir of his debt and left a life annuity of 12,000 francs to Charlotte Berthier, his companion since 1882.

financial situation, however, was worsening. Monet took up residence at Giverny.
Renoir abandoned the strict principles of Impressionism.

1884 Seurat, Signac, and Redon took part in the creation of the "Groupe des Artistes indépendants", whose purpose was to organize exhibitions without a screening before a jury nor the aim of winning an award. Guillaumin was alone among the original Impressionists to join this new group. Seurat exhibited *Bathing at Asnières*. The "Société des XX" was created in Brussels.

1885 Caillebotte painted a great deal less.

1885-1886 Victor Chocquet stopped buying new paintings.

1886 Took part in an exhibition organized in the United States by Durand-Ruel.

1886 Eighth and last Impressionist exhibition, which claimed to from free of the influence of dealers and the Salon. Monet, Renoir, Sisley, and Caillebotte did not take part. It featured 17 artists, among them Cassatt (7 works), Degas (5 paintings and 10 pastel drawings), Gauguin (19 works), Guillaumin (21 works), Morisot (12 paintings and a series of drawings and watercolors), Pissarro (12 paintings and a series of woodprints). The latter invited Seurat and Signac to join the group; Seurat showed 6 paintings, among them *A Sunday Afternoon on the Island of Grande Jatte* and 3 drawings, and Signac, 15 paintings and 3 drawings.
Durand-Ruel's exhibition of Impressionist paintings at the American Art Association received very favorable notice.

1887 His brother Martial married. Caillebotte took up residence at Petit-Gennevilliers. There he could indulge his two passions: gardening and boating.
He returned to Paris regularly and was a of the motivating force in the monthly literary and artistic dinners at the Café Riche.

1887 Durand-Ruel organized an exhibition in Brussels which made a great impression on the "Groupe des XX".
Monet and Renoir put on the yearly international exhibition at Georges Petit's, including works by Morisot, Sisley, and Pissarro. This was the most representative exhibition of the group since the Impressionist exhibition of 1882.

1888 Was elected to the municipal council of Petit-Gennevilliers.
It may have been through his friendship with Signac that he was invited to exhibit with the "Groupe des XX" in Brussels.

1889 New codicil to his will, which confirmed the previous provisions and left a house at Petit-Gennevilliers to Charlotte Berthier.
He contributed to the subscription to acquire Manet's Olympia.

1889-1890 Monet organized a subscription to acquire Manet's Olympia on behalf of the national collection.

1891 Seurat died.

1892 For the first time, the national collection bought a painting by Renoir.

1893 Showed more interest in painting.

1894 Caillebotte died on February 21 after a short illness. A commemorative exhibition was held at Durand-Ruel's.
He bequeathed 69 works to the state and only 40 were accepted – after great hesitations and thanks to Renoir's insistence: 2 paintings by Cézanne, 7 pastel drawings by Degas, 2 paintings by Manet, 8 paintings by Monet, 7 paintings by Pissarro, 6 paintings by Renoir, 6 paintings by Sisley, 1 watercolor and 1 drawing by Millet.

1894 Another major collector of Impressionist works died the same year, Dr. de Bellio.

Sailboats at Argenteuil
Ca 1885-1890
Oil on canvas
25⅝" × 21⅝" (65 × 55 cm)
Musée d'Orsay, Paris
Photo Réunion des
Musées nationaux, Paris

Bibliography

Catalogue raisonné

BERHAUT, Marie. *Caillebotte, sa vie et son œuvre* Catalogue raisonné of paintings and works in pastels. Paris: Bibliothèque des arts, 1977.

Selected bibliography

BALANDA, Marie-Josèphe de. *Gustave Caillebotte*. Lausanne: Edita 1988.

BERHAUT, Marie. *La Vie et l'œuvre de Gustave Caillebotte*. Paris, 1951. Int. by D. Wildenstein.

Caillebotte, the Impressionist. Lausanne: International Art Book, 1968. Trad. par Diana Imber.

CHARDEAU, Jean. *Les Dessins de Caillebotte*. Paris : Hermé, 1989.

DURANTY, Edmond. *La nouvelle peinture: à propos du groupe d'artistes qui expose dans les galeries Durand-Ruel*. Paris: Dentu, 1876. New ed. with foreword and notes by Marcel Guérin, Paris: Floury, 1946.

DURET, Théodore. *Histoire des peintres impressionnistes*. Paris, 1906.

FABERMAN, Hilarie. *Gustave Caillebotte 1875-1880*. Unpublished Master's thesis, Queens College, New York, 1975.

GEFFROY, Gustave. *Claude Monet, sa vie, son œuvre*. 2 vols. Paris: Crès, 1922. New revised ed. Pres. by Claudie Jufrin. Paris: Macula, 1980.

HUYSMANS, J.-K. *L'Art moderne*. Paris, 1883.

MOFFET, Charles ed. *The New painting : Impressionism 1874-1886*. Exhibition catalogue. The Fine Arts Museums of San Francisco, National Gallery of Art, Washington, D.C., 1986.

NOCHLIN, Linda. *Realism*. Harmondsworth, 1971.

REWALD, John. *The History of Impressionism*. 4th revised ed. New York: The Museum of Modern Art, 1973.

VARNEDOE, Kirk. *Gustave Caillebotte*. New Haven, Conn., London: Yale University Press, 1987.

WITTMER, Pierre. *Caillebotte au jardin : La période d'Yerres (1860-1879)*. Saint-Rémy-en-L'Eau: Monelle Hayot, 1990.

ZOLA, Émile. *Le bon combat de Courbet aux impressionnistes. Anthologie d'écrits sur l'art*, ed. by Gaëtan Picon. Paris: Savoir/Hermann, 1974.

Exhibitions

1951 *Gustave Caillebotte*. Retrospective exhibition. Galerie des Beaux-Arts, Paris.
Gustave Caillebotte. Wildenstein & Cie., Paris. Text by Marie Berhaut.

1965 *Caillebotte et ses amis impressionnistes*. Musée de Chartres. Foreword by Georges Besson.

1966 *Gustave Caillebotte*. Wildenstein & Co., London. Cat. by Denys Sutton.

1968 *Gustave Caillebotte*. Wildenstein & Co., New York.

1976-1977 *Gustave Caillebotte. A retrospective exhibition*. Museum of Fine Arts, Houston; Brooklyn Museum, New York. Cat. by J. Kirk Varnedoe and Thomas E. Lee.

1984 *Gustave Caillebotte 1848-1894*. Musée de Pontoise, Pontoise. Cat. by Edda Maillet.

1989 *Gustave Caillebotte 1848-1894*. Drawings, studies, and paintings. Galerie Brame et Lorenceau, Paris. Cat. by Pierre Wittmer.

1994-1995 *Gustave Caillebotte*. Musée d'Orsay, Paris; The Art Institute, Chicago.

List of illustrations

Acknowledgments

We wish to thank the owners of the works reproduced herein, as well as those who preferred to remain anonymous. We are grateful to the Wildenstein Galleries in New York and Galerie Schmit in Paris for their assistance. Also we owe deep gratitude to Galerie Brame et Lorenceau in Paris for their invaluable help in the making of this book.